RENDER UNTO CAESAR

Contents

1   A Personal Introduction   7
2   Defining Terms   11
3   The Bible on Government   17
4   Downhill from Constantine   29
5   The Responsible Citizen   41
6   Limits to Obedience   52
7   Party Politics   65
8   Pornography, Perversion and Censorship   75
9   Crime, Punishment and the Death Penalty   87
10   War   101
11   The Welfare State   113
    Notes   123

I

A Personal Introduction

One of my earliest ventures in writing was a booklet with the title *The Christian and the State*. Reviewers were kind, which is always good for a budding author's morale. It was however only a tentative beginning. It may seem to some that it has taken a long time for me to attempt something more extended. There were however reasons for the long delay—some of which, I trust, were due not just to my own failures but to the providence of God.

I am not referring now to the kind of pressure which besets the average pastor who has to fit in his writing with a multitude of other demands. Nor am I speaking of other books which became a priority as far as writing was concerned and have since been dispatched to the reading public. It was rather that I needed to learn a great deal more before I could embark again on the subject.

Those needed lessons came not only from books and discussions with friends. They were learned in the first place very painfully as I tried to hammer out my ideas in the context of my own personal struggles as a clergyman of the Church of England 'as by law established'. They were further developed by my removal to a pastorate in Northern Ireland just over a year before the beginning of what was to develop into years of trouble and violence. During this period I visited South Africa on six occasions, and experiences there certainly gave further food for deep reflection.

Let me first turn to my struggles of conscience as an Anglican parson. I was constantly faced with the issue of the relationship between church and state. It was not simply because of the presence of bishops in the House of Lords, the overriding control of the appointment of bishops by the Prime Minister, or the necessary approval of any developments in worship by a very mixed body of people, namely the House of Commons. It impinged on me at the local level by virtue of my position as vicar of the parish. At my induction I had sworn my oath of loyalty to the Queen as the supreme governor of the Church of England. I had to keep dutifully to a Prayer Book which was really an appendage to an act of parliament—the Act of Uniformity of 1662. I had to recognise as church people all and sundry who lived within the parish boundaries and who, by virtue of the fact that they lived within the realm of England, were to be treated in some sense as Christians, and therefore entitled to the sacraments and privileges of the state church, even though their attachment might be of the most nominal character. I was constantly reminded that I was part of a body which was from one point of view an ecclesiastical institution and from another a national English institution.

I have often been asked why I resigned from the ministry of the Church of England. My answer is twofold. First of all, there is the absurd anomaly that because of the quirks in parliamentary legislation of 1870 and 1871[1] I am not able to resign. So technically, by law, I have been an Anglican priest pastoring free church congregations for over twenty years. The more fundamental answer to the question is that I was forced by what I believed was the doctrine of the New Testament, to distinguish between the church as I saw it there, namely a company of believers, and the church as it appeared in the Anglican establishment—the religious side of the coin of national life!

I had, however, more lessons to learn. They came as I battled with the issues which confronted me and so many others in the developing tragedy of Northern Ireland, when I went there in 1967 to spend over fourteen years as pastor of a Baptist church. It was in some ways a very different situation, in that theoretically there was no established church, as the Anglican Church had been dis-established by Gladstone back in 1871. In fact there are three major groupings, each of which acts as if it is thus established. The Anglicans still behave as if 1871 had never happened—they are still in their view 'The Church of Ireland'. The four different bodies of Presbyterians are so firmly linked with their Scottish past that the ethos of the state establishment of the Church of Scotland still colours their thinking and attitude. On the other side of the great divide is Roman Catholicism for which the Virgin Mary is Queen of the Gaels and for which Ireland is a Catholic country suffering from the fact that religious outsiders came as colonists from England and Scotland in the seventeenth century. Behind the political, economic and cultural divisions which have rent Northern Ireland asunder, is the religious divide between those who want 'a Protestant parliament for a Protestant people' and those who dream of an Ireland united in Catholic identity. The issue of church and state is no theoretical one. It lies behind many an act of bloody violence.

To visit South Africa, as I did on various occasions, was to see the same issues. In Ulster it was the Protestant defending his religious heritage against Rome, and not always being too choosy about the means of defence. In South Africa it was the white man defending what he claimed to be Christian civilisation against the insidious surge of godless communism, even though it meant blatant injustice as part of the defence. Again there is the same mentality—God's own people in God's country fighting for the survival of what is seen as Christian culture and values.

It was all so reminiscent not only of Ulster but of the underlying pattern of English religious thinking ever since in the sixteenth century Richard Hooker wrote that 'there is no member of the Church of England who is not also a member of the commonwealth and no member of the commonwealth who is not also a member of the Church of England'. Indeed, the fallacy has even deeper roots in a far distant past. It was in the fourth century that one of the most disastrous wrong turnings of Christian history was taken. It was then that the churches which, as companies of believers in Jesus Christ who had faced bitter persecution from the Roman emperors, moved into a new climate of popular acceptance as they became the objects of imperial favour under the emperor Constantine. They were, before long, to become partners with the empire before finally merging into the amalgam of the religious and the political which has left us such a sad legacy.

So I try to write this book not in some theoretical fashion, but with my roots firmly in Scripture, my correctives in the recollection of some of the lessons of Christian history, and with my own involvement at the level of one individual tackling those great issues.

2

Defining Terms

If two people are to have a discussion or a debate, there must be basic agreement on the topic. This means that the key words which are the focus of the exchange must have a meaning accepted by both sides—otherwise they are talking at cross purposes as the same words are being used in different senses and the whole process becomes an exercise in futility. The relationship of an author to his readers is not quite the same as that between two people engaged in a debate. For one thing the reader is unable—exasperating as it may sometimes be—to reply to the argument, unless he happens to be writing a book review! It is all the more important, therefore, that an author clears the ground at the outset by making plain—or as clear as he can, which is a very different matter—what meaning he is giving to the basic words or theme of his book. In this book, the fundamental word is 'state'. What then is the sense in which I am using the word?

The problem is that it is easy to make clear the meaning of words which are concrete, but it is a great deal more difficult when they are abstract. Thus, if I was writing a book on aspects of farming and the title was simply 'Dairy Cows', it would be patently obvious what I was aiming to discuss. If, on the other hand, I was writing on genetic engineering in breeding, I would need to give a more detailed explanation of the theme. So, to write on a clearly defined concrete theme like England or France, would need little explanation; but to write on the theme of British or French jurisdiction is to move into the area of the abstract, and this requires a much more precise definition of terms.

To add to the problem, there is the fact that many people use a word or hear it used without giving too much, if any, thought to its meaning. How many people carrying British passports pause to ask what the title 'Principal Secretary of State' signifies? How many who read complaints in the press about state interference in press freedom give a second thought to the state which is alleged to be doing the interfering? There may be a vague feeling that it is another way of describing the government. But what the precise meaning of the word is tends to be left in the area of unexplored ideas. So, let's turn to exploration!

In many countries, the word 'state' is not used in the official designation. It may be a kingdom or a republic or a union of soviet republics. But behind the particular designation which deals more with the secondary sense of what precise form of constitutional arrangement prevails, is the underlying notion of the state. In the case of the United States of America that title becomes more explicit. Yet whether explicitly used or not, the basic character of any country is that it is a state.

It is obvious that state and nation are not interchangeable terms. The end of the second world war left the one German nation divided into two states with very different and at times mutually antagonistic systems. In India, many nations with different languages and cultures co-exist in one state. Then again there are nations like the Kurds who have no constitutional identity but are divided among three different states. The term 'nation' normally applies to a people with a common language and culture. The word 'state', while it is often closely linked with the word 'nation', is yet quite distinct.

A distinction may be useful in reaching a conclusion about the meaning of the word 'state'. The word 'nation' may be said to be a concrete term. It consists of actual physical bodies since it comprises the sum total of living people at any given time who share an ethnic or linguistic identity. The term 'state' is however abstract and, as we have already commented, it is notoriously more difficult to define abstract words than concrete ones.

It may be helpful to compare another very familiar community word, namely 'school'. We may apply this to the building, but only in a limited sense, for the building may be extensively altered and indeed may be totally destroyed and the site re-developed, and yet the essential school continues. Nor may we limit the notion of a school by applying it to the staff and pupils, for they are constantly changing and yet a generation later the school remains.

In fact we mean a particular community organised in a specific way with its board of governors, its authorised staff members, and its rules for admission or expulsion, its code of behaviour, etc. In short, it is a structured community with its own laws governing its life and activities.

The analogy may well be applied. The state is an organised or structured community. The structures may be very simple, as in the case of a jungle tribe in the Western Amazon, or they may be highly complex, as in a modern technological society. The regime may have a single authoritarian head, whether tribal chief or military dictator. It may be a constitutional monarchy or a democratic republic. It may be governed by a cabinet system or by a party presidium. Indeed there may be a military coup or a revolution or a civil war with a resulting complete change in the pattern of government. Yet in every case there is a basic similarity. The community, whether the small tribe or the very large nation or group of nations, is bound together by a common submission to a supreme authority where, to use a famous or perhaps notorious phrase of a former US president Richard Nixon: 'The buck stops here.'

To have a governing authority and a people who are governed implies a system of laws. The laws are made, modified, or revoked by the leader or the council of leaders who have the final authority. Laws are however not mere expressions of a government's wishes which may or may not be heeded. The income tax demand in the buff envelope is not in the same category as the charitable appeal. The police sign 'No parking' carries an insistence which cannot be asserted by the private citizen whose garden gate is often blocked.

Since laws are not only promulgated but enforced, the governing body must have the means to see that this is done. In a small tribe this can be enforced by a tribal gathering which punishes the offender. In a large country this is clearly impossible. Hence there is a police force, and law courts which impose fines or imprisonment—in short, the whole complex judicial system which sees to it that as far as possible the governed will conform to the formulated decisions of the government.

To administer any community, whether a family, a club or a country, requires financial resources. In the case of a government's need for money, the requirement is issued within the context of authority, so the demand carries the ultimate threat of fines or imprisonment if taxes are not paid. Taxes may irk the citizen, and in fact they may at times be unreasonably harsh. The feebleness or even the corruption of the government may be obvious. Yet unless the social structures are to disintegrate into anarchy, the taxes must be paid. Furthermore, if they are to be levied then the state authorities must know who its citizens are and where they live. Hence there is the regular scrutiny of national life by means of a census. Such a census is in a totally different category from market sampling or opinion polls. It is not dependent on the goodwill or the co-operation of the citizens. Like all else within the state's jurisdiction, it is enforceable by laws administered by the police and the courts.

Such authority is limited geographically. Just as at a local level parents have authority over their own children but not over the children next door, so a government has jurisdiction only over those within its own national boundaries. That is why the process of extradition has to be applied if one of its citizens commits a crime and escapes to another country. A national police force cannot cross a frontier and arrest someone who is now under another government's jurisdiction.

Human nature however, being what it is, there will be disagreements as to the limits of jurisdiction. One country will smoulder with resentment that part of what is viewed as national territory has been appropriated in the past by others. A nation which is bursting at the seams within its own confines may cast covetous eyes on the wide open spaces, or the mineral wealth, or the strategic value of part of another state's territory. It is out of such disagreements that wars emerge.

To sum up, a state is a community whether small or large where there is a recognised governing authority, a code of laws and the resources to see that those laws are enforced. When the government is extremely weak, or when there is a breakdown of law and order or worse still civil war, then there is no longer a stable state but anarchy. It is the presence of law and order declared and enforced which is the essential characteristic of a state.

The Christian however has to take into account another major consideration. To be born again means entry into the kingdom of heaven. Paul describes the radical change effected by conversion—God 'has rescued us from the dominion of darkness and brought us into the kingdom of the Son he loves' (Col 1:13). He makes quite explicit the implications as far as citizenship is concerned as he writes to the Philippians. They were in a garrison town where the legionaries of the Roman empire guarded the frontier. They were vividly aware of the privilege of being a Roman citizen. Paul was also deeply conscious of his own personal privilege in that he could say, 'I am a Roman citizen.' Yet here he reminds his Philippian readers and significantly identifies himself with them: 'Our citizenship is in heaven. And we eagerly await a Saviour from there, the Lord Jesus Christ' (Phil 3:20). This means that at one and the same time the Christian is a citizen of heaven and a citizen of a particular earthly state. He then has civic responsibilities which draw him in two directions.

This raises the possibility of a clash of loyalties if the demands of the earthly rulers should conflict with those of the heavenly King. It was this tension which lay behind the words of Jesus: 'Give to Caesar what is Caesar's, and to God what is God's' (Mt 22:21). It also lay behind the firm response of the disciples under pressure from the Jewish leaders: 'Judge for yourselves whether it is right in God's sight to obey you rather than God' (Acts 4:19). Peter and John had no doubt in their own minds where their primary loyalty lay. The plain implication of their question is that if rulers were truly just and were honestly fulfilling their God-given role, they would not impose on the citizens of the King of kings demands which would conflict with the Christian's civic loyalty. It is however a sad fact that all too often the earthly rules either ignore or defy the heavenly King. It is this that has led again and again to persecution and to suffering for Christ's sake. It has led also to heart searching and serious discussion among Christians as to the nature of civic responsibility and the limits of such obedience. The tensions which arise lie behind the writing of this book.

3

The Bible on Government

The basic starting point in all our knowledge of God is the revelation in the opening verses of Genesis that God is the Creator. Everything exists by virtue of his creative power. All that continues to exist does so because of his sustaining power. This applies not only to the physical universe but to all living beings whether demonic or human. As the Creator who brought them into existence and who sustains them in being, God has absolute authority to which all are answerable and all must finally submit.

The basic doctrine of the Bible which expresses this fundamental truth is the sovereignty of God Almighty. He alone has an underived life. He alone is totally independent of any other being or circumstance. He alone is entirely self-sufficient. He is the source of all things, the sustainer of all and the goal of all. Paul sums it up in one glorious burst of praise: 'From him and through him and to him are all things. To him be the glory for ever! Amen' (Rom 11:36).

It is obvious that this sovereignty has not gone unchallenged. Indeed a superficial judgement might conclude that the challenge has been relatively successful in view of the widespread ignoring or defiance of his sovereign rights by men and women. Such an assessment however fails to recognise two truths which God has revealed; namely that all rebellion against his authority is only tolerated for the present by his permission, and furthermore it is only permitted during the temporary period before time gives way to eternity.

What about Satan, someone may object? Is he not designated in the New Testament by Jesus himself as 'the prince of this world' (Jn 12:31)? In John's first letter is there not the further acknowledgement that the whole world is under the control of the evil one (1 Jn 5:19)? However, the opening chapter of Job shows very clearly that Satan can only operate within the restrictions imposed by the Sovereign God. Furthermore, Jesus' reference to the prince of this world is in the context of his announcement of his coming victory on the cross (Jn 14:28–30). John, in his vision on the island of Patmos, was given a glimpse of the celestial conflict, but it was with the assurance that 'our Lord God Almighty reigns' (Rev 19:6). The venomous resistance by the devil is set against the background of his realisation that 'his time is short' (Rev 12:12).

Thus, the coming of Jesus is declared by John the Baptist and by Jesus himself as the coming of the kingdom. This must not be viewed as a heroic attempt to establish God's sovereignty against overwhelming odds. Rather it is the arrival of God's long-prepared hour—'when the time had fully come' (Gal 4:4). The bridgehead established in rebel territory was not some forlorn hope. Rather it was the first stage of the open disclosure of what was always true, namely that the Lord reigns. In the present ordering of history, and fully in accordance with the purposes of God, this kingdom is only recognised by the people of God who in repentance and faith have turned to the Saviour. They are however fully persuaded that they are 'more than conquerors' (Rom 8:37). Thus, when they pray in the Lord's prayer: 'Your Kingdom come,' it is with the assurance that it has already come in the experience of the people of God, but yet awaits its final public consummation when the King returns in person and every knee shall bow and every tongue confess that Jesus Christ is Lord (Phil 2:10–11).

Every consideration of the nature and purpose of the state must be rooted in the biblical conviction that the Lord is the ultimate source of all authority and that every rebellion, whether demonic or human, is inevitably temporary and doomed to final defeat. The arrogance of men, and especially of those who reach positions of authority, must be seen as subject to the supreme authority of the Most High God.

Nebuchadnezzar had to learn that lesson the hard way. It was in the eclipse of his power and the loss of his reason, both mercifully restored by God, that he was forced to recognise that 'the Most High is sovereign over the kingdoms of men and gives them to anyone he wishes' (Dan 4:32). Earlier, the psalmist had given an inspired comment on the arrogance of the rulers of the nations who try to defy God: 'The One enthroned in heaven laughs; the Lord scoffs at them. Then he rebukes them in his anger and terrifies them in his wrath, saying , "I have installed my King on Zion, my holy hill"' (Ps 2:4–6). The wise commentator, well taught by the Spirit of God, reveals the same truth when he records the words of God's wisdom: 'By me kings reign and rulers make laws that are just; by me princes govern, and all nobles who rule on earth' (Prov 8:15–16).

The opening chapters of Genesis however not only reveal the Sovereign God, the Creator and Sustainer of all things, they also reveal the necessary implications of that sovereignty in the demands he made on the man and the woman he created. Those demands were not the harsh edicts of some arbitrary despot. The fact that they were issued in the context of an earthly paradise overflowing in such generous provision indicates that they were the demands of a loving and caring Creator and that as a result they are for the good of his creatures.

Genesis however not only reveals God in his sovereign power and gracious care, but also shows the nature of man as he came fresh from the hand of his Creator, and also the ugly character of his rebellion against that same Creator, and the tragic consequences, not only in terms of his own moral deterioration, but of his relationships with his fellows. Man as originally created was and always will be a social being. Social values and human relationships are not the evidence of long centuries of development. We adjust to living with others because that is the way God made us. We fail to relate to others, and we behave in anti-social ways because that is what sin has done to us.

The very act of creation made men and women social beings.

The decision in heaven is recorded for our instruction: 'Let us make man in our image, in our likeness' (Gen 1:26). It is not simply because of some quirk in the Hebrew language that the word 'God' is not in the singular but in the plural. The God who revealed himself in the first dawn of human history was not some solitary deity set in a state of eternal loneliness. He was God in company, God who embraced within his life the richness of three persons all sharing the same divine life. Mysterious it is to our finite minds; yet it is a rich warm truth for it tells us that our God is a community being, sharing eternally in the mutual love and inter-related activity of the Father, the Son and the Holy Spirit.

It is not therefore a surprise that when God created Adam in his own likeness, he gave him an inbuilt gregarious instinct which required other human beings for its fulfilment. So when the Triune God commented on this complex being whom he had created: 'It is not good for the man to be alone' (Gen 2:18), he was simply saying that a being made in the likeness of the God whose life involves fellowship will also need fellows. Hence the next necessary and indeed inevitable step was for God to create Eve (hence also the command to them both to be fruitful). Human history thus began not only with a man and a woman related together, but with the source of their life in a God who himself lives by divine relationships sustained in love.

When Adam and Eve disobeyed God they were not only flouting their Creator's word, they were also violating their own nature. Their fall not only corrupted them within their own being, but produced a sense of shame which was like a shadow on their relationship. The next sorry step was inevitable as another relationship was destroyed by hatred and then by murder when Cain killed his own brother. The slope had already become steep with all the future tragic consequences in cruelty, exploitation, theft, murder and war.

The situation cried out not only for laws to curb men's lawlessness, but for sanctions and penalties to back up those laws. The necessity for a socially-cohesive force to restrain human sinfulness was implicit in the deteriorating situation. God's answer was the social sanction and so the restraints of the family, the community and the state. The ultimate answer would be the coming of God himself to establish his irresistible authority, and then at the end of history to usher in the final glory of the kingdom. Until that glory dawned, and while human passions were still rampant, all the divinely-given sanctions would be needed if social life was to have even a faint echo of its original design.

The ugly reality of human sinfulness has another implication for our understanding of the nature of the state. It is that every human institution is inevitably imperfect. The finest political theory, and the attempts to embody it in law and to carry it out in practice, are all alike affected by the fundamental and inescapable fact that political thinkers, rulers and citizens are sinners. This means that human selfishness will continually intrude to spoil even the best schemes. Men have dreamed of a utopia with wise rulers and contented citizens. Plato, the great philosopher of ancient Greece, had such a vision when he wrote *The Republic*. Thomas More in the sixteenth century had the same hope when he wrote his *Utopia*, Karl Marx had a similar dazzling prospect—in his case it was to be the classless society.

Sadly, every attempt has ended in disillusionment. The ideal ruler turns out to be power hungry, or greedy, or immoral. The administration not only produces devoted servants, but also corruption, selfish ambition and bitter division. The people are like their rulers, aiming by and large at self-interest and personal advantage. The kingdoms of this world will always give evidence of the essential sinfulness of their people until the final triumph of the King. Only then will they become 'the kingdom of our Lord and of his Christ, and he will reign for ever and ever' (Rev 11:15).

It is the fact of universal sinfulness attested both in Scripture (Rom 3:23) and in experience which produces the necessity of law being imposed. God himself wrote his law on the conscience of every man (Rom 2:15) and has spelled out that law in more specific detail in the Scriptures. Where he delegates his authority to human beings, whether to parents in a family or rulers in a nation, they also exercise that authority by means of law. It may not be designated as law in a home, yet the code of behaviour which is expected has the essential characteristics of law in that it sets boundary lines for conduct, imposes penalties and gives rewards.

In the running of the affairs of the nation there is the legal declaration of the accepted pattern of behaviour. It is enforced by the police so that it is not mere exhortation. It is backed by the courts with their sanctions of fines or imprisonment. At every level there is a recognition that human beings have to be compelled to behave in a socially acceptable way. They have to be restrained from following their own ambitions or lusts at the expense of others. The ruler, writes Paul, 'is God's servant to do you good. But if you do wrong, be afraid, for he does not bear the sword for nothing. He is God's servant, an agent of wrath to bring punishment on the wrongdoer' (Rom 13:45).

This passage brings into focus the positive function of the ruler, namely 'to do you good'. The restraint of wickedness and the punishment of crime are not merely negative reactions. They are intensely positive in that they are the necessary sanctions in order to ensure for the citizens at large the stability of a social structure which makes normal life possible. Thus the existence of the state as a God-given institution highlights another biblical principle, namely the grace of God.

A traditional distinction drawn by Christian theologians is helpful here. It is that between the common and the special grace of God. By the latter we refer to the redeeming work of Christ by which sinners are saved from the penalty of sin, kept by God's power from its tyranny and finally delivered from its very presence. But God is not only specially gracious to those who respond in repentance and faith to the call of the gospel. He has also a general benevolence towards all men in spite of their rebellion against him. Jesus summed up the wonderful impartiality of God's common grace: 'He causes his sun to rise on the evil and the good, and sends rain on the righteous and the unrighteous' (Mt 5:45).

The state is thus a gracious provision instituted by the God of grace. Knowing his creatures as he does, and knowing the intolerable anarchy which would be the inevitable outcome of unbridled sinfulness, he has set a check upon men and women. The laws of the state are human enactments and therefore themselves suffer from the moral imperfection implicit in every human scheme or achievement. Yet in so far as they restrain crime and anti-social activity, they make normal living possible. They are in fact a gracious restraint imposed on the wilder passions of men in order that people in general may enjoy peace. That is why in Romans 13 Paul links the terror of the legal sanctions of the state with the positive social advantages. The ruler is not only appointed to check evil but to 'do you good'. That is also why Paul urges Timothy to pray for rulers. It is that 'we may live peaceful and quiet lives in all godliness and holiness' (1 Tim 2:2).

Admittedly the ruler may fall far short of the ideal, but so also may a father. Yet the sad fact that there are vicious, drunken and cruel fathers does not abrogate the general principle that authority over the family unit is a divine ordinance. No more does the existence of evil rulers cancel the basic principle that the governing authorities are ordained by God. There is an old principle that abuse does not cancel use, and certainly that applies in this case. Even bad government is superior to the chaos of general anarchy. Weak rulers and wicked rulers may discharge their responsibilities in feeble or self-serving ways, yet they still constitute a divinely-ordained authority to whom citizens owe loyal obedience. In spite of the many perversions of political power, the Bible constantly re-affirms the same pattern in which the divinely-ordained ruler acts with authority, providing for his people's welfare, controlling blatant evil-doers, and promoting general social harmony.

In considering the developing teaching of Scripture, it should be noted that the Old Testament does not present a precisely-formulated political scheme. Rather it describes personal relationship situations in which ruler and ruled interact. Benevolent rule is praised, and evil regimes are castigated. God remains gracious in his dealings with men and women—even in the face of their wilful and persistent rebellion against him. So he still works in providence to set them within national communities where law and order make normal living and working possible.

The major feature in the Old Testament in its survey of the nations is the distinction between the people of God and the nations in general. With some notable exceptions like Ruth or Naaman, the people of God are embodied in one nation, Israel. Beyond the boundaries of Israel are the nations who may be friendly to Israel or bitterly hostile. They are nonetheless outside the covenant people.

At one point however Israel and the nations stand together, and that is before the judgement of God. Thus a prophet like Amos castigates not only Israel, but Edom, Syria, Moab and others, where they are guilty of violation of the moral law. Israel, because of her greater privilege, comes under a more severe censure, but every national leader faces the same Judge. It was for example a Babylonian king who heard the final indictment coming through the prophet Daniel: 'You have been weighed on the scales and found wanting' (Dan 5:27).

Within Israel there is a constant reminder that the Lord is King. Indeed, the king ruling over the nation is seen as the Lord's representative. Jehovah is the real ruler, but his kingly authority is represented in visible form in a man of flesh and blood. So the king is called 'the Lord's anointed' because he has been designated by the Lord as the one who embodies in his person the final authority of Jehovah. Even before the days of the monarchy the same pattern was evident. Thus Moses was directly appointed by the Lord. The Judges are referred to again and again as being raised up by God and sent to their authoritative task. With Saul and David, the first two kings, God's direct intervention and anointing are made quite explicit.

Israel was God's commonwealth. Here there was to be a glimpse of the vanished glory of a creation order with a community subject to its Creator. Yet the vision was sadly blurred both by national apostasy and by the recurring failure of the kings to be in fact what they were in title—'the Lord's anointed'. It was out of this dual failure that the prophetic testimony emerged with increasing clarity. In place of a failed monarchy there will come God's true King, the Messiah. In face of a backsliding and degenerate nation there will be a kingdom which will not display the seemingly inevitable brief history before inexorable decline sets in. Rather it will be the kingdom of Daniel's vision—an everlasting kingdom which will finally eclipse and destroy all other merely human rule and authority.

It is with this prophetic background, and indeed with the long history of Israel as the foil to display God's purposes, that we can appreciate the preaching of John the Baptist with which the New Testament opens: 'Repent for the kingdom of heaven is near' (Mt 3:2). John stood at the close of the old era and on the threshold of the new. The messianic King so long expected was about to be revealed.

John's teaching was very soon taken up by Jesus himself. No longer was the messianic King the expected one. The Lord came in person. He had come to challenge the usurper whom Jesus himself designated as 'the prince of this world'. Satan's long usurpation was coming to an end. The new kingdom would be like the salient established by the allied armies in the second world war on the Normandy beaches, and which sounded the death knell of Hitler's reign, and led to its final collapse. So the Messiah could declare that the kingdom had come, and yet tell his disciples to pray for its coming. It had come in that the messianic King had come to conquer. It had yet to come in the sense that the final overthrow of 'the prince of this world' would await the Second Coming of the victorious Saviour.

To say that there is a major difference between the Old Testament and the New would seem to be so obvious as to require no comment. Indeed, some readers might almost feel insulted by the apparent suggestion that this glaringly obvious fact might not be known to them. Yet this so obvious truth has in fact been sadly misunderstood down the centuries, and is still being misunderstood. Listen to people in Britain or the USA talking about a Christian country, or Northern Ireland Protestants contending for a Protestant people, or South African whites eulogising God's country and you discover that the blindness is widespread.

Certainly Christians have seen the difference between the two testaments in the area of ministry. You cannot read the Epistle to the Hebrews without seeing that the Levitical priesthood with its many animal sacrifices has given way to the high-priestly work of Jesus who has offered the one sufficient sacrifice.

Again, many can see the difference between the forward-looking revelation of the Old Testament writers and the complete revelation of the New. The opening verse of the same letter to the Hebrews sets this out with magnificent clarity: 'In the past God spoke to our forefathers through the prophets at many times and in various ways, but in these last days he has spoken to us by his Son.' Jesus is God's final Word. He is the great Prophet.

Yet in spite of their fully justified protests against Rome's priestly view of the ministry and Rome's open-ended view of revelation which is supplemented by the authoritative teaching of the church, Protestants have often failed to see their own inconsistency. They have seen Jesus fulfil the messianic offices of Priest and Prophet, but have failed to see him as also fulfilling the office of King. Yet that is a vital element of the fulfilment of the work of the Messiah, and we must insist that not only does the New Testament view church life as new, but so also does it view national life.

In the Old Testament the people of God really meant Israel under the Lord's anointed. Now however the people of God are scattered across all the nations. 'There is neither Jew nor Greek' (Gal 3:28) within the church of Christ, for national distinctions have become secondary. Nor is the Lord's anointed any longer the king or ruler of one particular nation. Christ is King of all the nations, although as yet his kingly rule is willingly seen and gladly accepted only within his church. In this kingdom the citizens are not members by national pedigree, nor by virtue of conquest. They are members because of the new birth (Jn 3:3–5).

Certain conclusions seem clear, though tragically they have been sadly obscured. In the first place there is not, and indeed cannot be, such a thing as 'a Christian country'. Nor can there be such a person as 'a Christian ruler'. It is true that there can be a country with very many Christians. There can be a nation in which generations of Christians have influenced both laws and culture. But in neither case does this make the nation or its constitutional arrangements especially sacred. It is simply that in that nation the messianic King has pushed the frontiers of his kingdom much further into enemy territory.

Nor can there be in the Old Testament sense a Christian king. Certainly there may be a king, queen or president who is a true believer and who endeavours to influence national life. But the Christian head of state is never in the same role as the Old Testament king. It is here that the great reformation confessions like the Thirty Nine Articles or the Westminster Confessions go astray. 'The magistrate' has no more rights within the church than any other member. He is a believer in a very influential position in the state. That position however gives no special rights within the church.

In the New Testament, the state is not seen as being the constitutional aspect of the church. Nothing could be more remote from the New Testament view than the famous dictum of Richard Hooker quoted earlier. State and church are quite distinct. There is an overlap of course since members of the church are also citizens of the state. In the purposes of God however the roles of state and church are quite separate. The state is set by God to defend its citizens, to promote their welfare and to restrain evil-doers. The church is the dwelling place of the Spirit, the witness to the gospel and a school for Christian discipleship.

This very clear distinction continues throughout the New Testament between the people of God and the nations in which they live, between the citizens of the heavenly kingdom and the citizens of the earthly state. It is because they belong to two quite different realms that tensions and divided loyalties inevitably arise. In such situations the ultimate loyalty of the Christian is due to Christ the King.

After all, the state of which he is a citizen has a temporary existence—as do all earthly states. Only Christ's kingdom will last for ever. The kingly rule of Christ is seen now in his church where the members of the kingdom are gathered together by the

Holy Spirit. The church may be a minority group, and in some countries a tiny minority, yet it is there that ultimate power resides. It is there that the new kingdom has been established. It is there that the dawn of the final day has come—that day when the prophetic vision will be realised: 'The kingdom of the world has become the kingdom of our Lord and of his Christ, and he will reign for ever and ever' (Rev 11:15).

4

Downhill from Constantine

The earliest congregations of Christians came to birth in very hostile situations. The Acts of the Apostles recalls the initial clash between the young church in Jerusalem and the Jewish ruling classes where the Pharisees, who represented religious traditionalists, and the Sadducees, who were the high-priestly political class, combined in furious opposition to what they viewed as a heretical betrayal of Judaism.

The imperial authorities, seen through the eyes of the historian Luke as he wrote the Acts, appear again and again as the bulwark to guard Christian liberty. So the Roman centurion rescued Paul from the Jewish mob who were out to kill him. The tribune who provided an armed escort to conduct him to Caesarea saved him from assassination by Jewish fanatics. The apostle felt free and confident to make his dramatic appeal to be judged at the court of Caesar in Rome. Consistently the state authorities appear in their God-given role as the defenders of the weak against a powerful religious lobby, or in the face of mob violence.

When, however, the gospel began to penetrate deeply into the life of the empire attitudes began to change. Like any dictators, the emperors were constantly on the alert for any movement which suggested subversion. The fact that the founder of this new religion had been executed by a Roman governor with the title 'King of the Jews' over the cross doubtless bred an initial uneasiness. The further fact that his followers claimed to be citizens of a new kingdom and to owe unconditional loyalty to their King Jesus, would mark them out as being even more suspect. Their refusal to join in what were looked on as normal social activities, such as idolatrous and immoral banquets, marked them out further as being in Roman eyes anti-social, and therefore potentially dangerous.

For a ruthless blackguard like the Emperor Nero it proved useful to have scapegoats whose brutal repression would divert popular attention from his own iniquities. Politicians have often been prone—and still are—to pounce on any diversionary occurence to shift attention from their own failures. If such a situation does not actually exist it is not too difficult to produce one.

It is not surprising therefore to find the early history of the Christian movement unfolding in a panorama of bloody and ruthless persecution. Peter in his first Epistle prepared his readers for the fierce testing ahead as he wrote: 'Now for a little while you may have had to suffer grief in all kinds of trials' (1 Pet 1:6). Already the storms of government opposition were beating on young churches. Those storms were to become widespread gales of such ferocity that the persecuted churches would surely have been destroyed had it not been for the supernatural power of the Christ who had promised: 'I will build my church, and the gates of Hades will not overcome it' (Mt 16:18).

It was to persecuted Christians in Asia Minor that the apostle John wrote the final book of the New Testament. The Apocalypse is, as the Greek title indicates, the unveiling or revelation of what is hidden. In this case the hidden element is the future with its attendant factor, namely the ultimate ending of human history. Men have always speculated about the future. The current craze for astrological predictions is only one more example of that innate human desire to probe the unseen. The Apocalypse, however, is not one further addition to the list of human speculations. Rather it is the divine unveiling of the ultimate conquest by Christ of every opposing force. The final victory will not only mean the eternal doom of the prince of this world and the overthrow of every hostile human power, it will also mean the eternal reign of Christ.

It was this vision of the ultimate triumph of the Redeemer

which was designed to strengthen the suffering saints in Asia Minor to whom John wrote from his own situation of suffering on the island of Patmos. It was that same vision which sustained an innumerable company of martyrs in the first three centuries of Christian history. The barbaric tortures and the terrible deaths in the arenas of Rome were faced with courage and with a remarkable peace which could only be described as supernatural. They had so glimpsed the coming glory of the reigning Saviour that neither the fading glories of imperial Rome nor the brutal persecution could influence them to deny their Lord. They were after all citizens not of a tottering empire, but of an everlasting kingdom which no power on earth or in hell could hope to overthrow.

The situation was unbelievably different within a few years of the beginning of the fourth century. The opening years of that century saw the fierce onslaught of the persecuting emperor, Diocletian. Under his successor Galerius 'the year 308 was a veritable "Year of Terror" and the severity of the trial lasted for two years longer'.[2] It must have seemed to the believers as if all hell had been let loose against them. It is not surprising therefore that many Christians breathed a sigh of relief and welcomed the new emperor Constantine. They probably never realised that their relief from suffering would be at the expense of the corrupting of churches and states for many centuries to come.

The decisive battle for the imperial crown of Rome was fought at the Milvian Bridge in AD 312. The claimant who was to prove the victor was Constantine. On the night before the battle he claimed to have seen a vision—a cross of light in the night sky with the words *in hoc signo vinces* (by this sign you will conquer). It was not surprising therefore that after his victory the new emperor issued an edict of toleration.

He recognised the remarkable spread of the Christian message so that in spite of nearly three centuries of recurring persecutions Christians were to be found everywhere and in all strata of society. The blood of the martyrs, to quote from a famous saying of Tertullian, had indeed become the seed of the church. Constantine faced a situation where there had been civil war with rival claimants to the throne, and where continuing tensions constantly threatened the disintegration of the empire. What was needed was a social cement to bind the empire together. What better agency for unity than the Christian churches!

In AD 323, legislation was introduced favouring the church, with tax concessions for the clergy which doubtless they welcomed. The inevitable slide towards an alliance of church and state had begun. By AD 363, under the emperor Jovian, only Christian worship was permitted and paganism which had formerly been the dominant pattern became the unacceptable religion. AD 383 saw the edict which forbade the renunciation of the Christian faith. By AD 391 the downhill path continued with the edict of the emperor Theodusius which not only prohibited pagan worship but declared that only the form of Christianity recognised by the emperor as orthodox would be tolerated. The fusion of church and state was complete!

It was all a far cry from the early days. Then the Christians had been the despised and persecuted minority, harried by successive emperors and yet not only surviving but spreading. Now the churches were popular. It became respectable and indeed the only safe option to declare yourself a Christian, and the officially-approved kind of Christian at that.

The consequences were tragic. Pagans flooded into the churches, bringing many of their ideas and practices with them. One can easily trace the later growth of the superstitions and errors which darkened the churches in the Middle Ages to this disastrous period. The preaching elder in the church was supplanted by the sacrificing priest. The simple communion meal of the early days became the sacrifice offered to propitiate God. The table for the Lord's Supper became the sacrificial altar. The mother goddess of the Mediterranean world was to reappear as the Madonna in the churches, just as the sacred shrines of paganism were to be refurbished as places of Christian pilgrimage.

Two of the most ugly results of the union of church and state were the secularising of the ministry, and the adoption by Christians of the methods of persecution from which their spiritual forefathers had suffered so greatly. For the preachers of the early centuries, a call to the ministry could mean a summons to a prison cell and a martyr's death. Now, however, the ministry was to be the door to a favoured and popular role. In the centuries ahead, worldly clerics would rise to positions of prominence in many a state. When the Roman empire itself collapsed the way was open for the papacy to emerge as the new imperial power which was to lead to the increasingly extravagant claims of the mediaeval popes.

Persecution, formerly the pagan instrument to try and crush the Christians, now became a weapon in the hands of church leaders. In the early days there was the recognition that only moral pressure and in extreme cases ex-communication were biblically authorised forms of discipline. Now, however, and increasingly as the centuries passed, civil procedures, imprisonment and the ultimate sanction of the death penalty became acceptable forms of religious coercion. The great Augustine capitulated to the sorry notion when, in face of his dispute with the Donatists whom he viewed as heretics, he misused the scriptural command: 'Make them come in' (Lk 14:23), as sanctioning the use of the power of the state against them. An even more chilling moment came in AD 385 in Spain when Priscillian was executed for alleged heresy. The wheel had turned full circle. The alliance of church and state had reached its inevitable and tragic conclusion.

During the long centuries of the Middle Ages the alliance was cemented. In AD 800 the emperor Charlemagne was crowned by the Pope in Rome. The notion of Christendom emerged in which citizenship of the empire and membership of the church became interchangable terms. There would be tensions, and at times open conflict, between popes and emperors, but it was simply in terms of who had the place of pre-eminence in the one sacral commonwealth.

Out of this unnatural and unbiblical union, further sad consequences flowed. There were the forced conversions of tribes and nations. The Saxons for example were baptised—not because of the impact of the gospel, but at the point of the sword. Thus baptised paganism was the platform for the launching of one of the most tragic movements in Christian history—the Crusades. These military attempts to muster the forces of Christendom in order to dislodge the 'infidel' Muslims from the so-called holy places in Jerusalem, were not only to prove militarily a failure, but were to leave a major hindrance to the evangelising of the Islamic Middle East which continues to this day.

When the great spiritual movement which is known as the Protestant Reformation swept Europe in the sixteenth century, it marked the beginning of a new era. Many of the superstitions and errors of the past were swept away. The Bible became the book of the common man, and the preaching of the gospel was heard far and wide with enormous blessing following. The Reformers challenged Rome both as to the pretensions of the papacy and to the many false doctrines which had crept into the teaching of the church. At one significant point, however, the Reformers failed to part company with Rome. It was in this deep-rooted belief in the alliance of church and state.

When Martin Luther made his historic protest and challenged the very foundations of Roman Catholicism, he failed to challenge this issue. Thus on the one hand he made his appeal to the German princes for support, and on the other he countenanced the persecution of those nick-named Anabaptists or rebaptisers. Their serious error in the eyes of both Protestants and Catholics was that they rejected the alliance of church and state because they believed that this produced huge national religious institutions rather than companies of committed believers. Yet it was the latter which they saw in the churches of the New Testament.

Luther's own doctrines pointed him in the same direction. Did he not insist that the sinner is justified by faith alone? Did he not restore to the church the New Testament doctrine of the priesthood of all believers? One can see his uneasiness in his development of the idea of the 'ecclesiola in ecclesia' (the little church within the church), that is, the true company of believers within the national ecclesiastical institution. It was an attempt to blend the facts of Scripture and spiritual experience on the one hand, with the pragmatic aim of the essentially conservative Luther to maintain the stability of German society. To go back on centuries of Constantinian compromise was too much.

Two sorry results soon followed—compromise never does solve real problems! On the one hand the Anabaptists met the combined fury of both Protestants and Catholics. There was a gathering of the German Princes at the Diet of Speyer in 1529 which produced the name Protestant because of their courageous protest against the attempt of the emperor Charles V to get them back into the Roman fold. Yet it was at that same gathering that both sides combined forces to issue the edict of Speyer which pronounced the death penalty on any who baptised someone who had been christened in infancy. The Catholics with long practice behind them excelled in the numbers of Anabaptists massacred, but sad to say the Protestants also played their part. Indeed the first Anabaptist martyrs to die were in the Protestant canton of Berne where there was another dominant figure, Zwingli, himself to die in a battle with Catholic forces.

The other result of the sad compromise was a further compromising principle which aimed to bring peace between the warring factions. It was the theory *cuius regio eius religio* (whatever the region is, that is the religion). So the ruler's religious preference was forced on his people. The ecclesiastical map of Europe was re-drawn with its Protestant nations and its Catholic ones. The resulting tragedy was the so-called wars of religion. The longer-term results were the settling down of national ecclesiastical organisations within their own frontiers. This led to a failure to make any real attempt to breach the entrenched ramparts of Rome in southern Europe for a very long time to come.

John Calvin, the other great leader of the Reformation, differed in his views at various points from Luther's position. He too, however, was committed to the same basic idea of the Christian nation and was ready to endorse the execution of the heretic Servetus. It has always seemed a weak defence that he urged the city council of Geneva to use the sword for execution rather than burning the heretic alive. The net result would have been the same! What is more significant is that Calvin had the solid support of so many of the Reformation leaders.

In England and Scotland the same underlying idea of the Christian nation was to prevail. In England it took an Episcopal form and in Scotland a Presbyterian. In England state control in the church was and still is much more pronounced. In both, however, the same Old Testament pattern is behind the differing formulations, namely that the ruler has a responsibility to maintain and defend the true religion.

In the English settlement, the crown in parliament has had the final authority in the Church of England. Thus the ultimate decision in appointing bishops lies with the Chief Minister of the Crown in no. 10 Downing Street, while changes in the pattern of worship have had to be sanctioned by parliament. There have been compensations in the appointment of bishops to the House of Lords and in all the varied ways in which the established church has special privileges. It was only in the last century that some of the final vestiges of actual repression of non-conformists were removed. Today we live in a pluralist society, but it is still with an established church, with the sovereign anointed and crowned in a religious ceremony, and with the pervasive notion which only tends to surface at times of national crisis that this is a Christian country.

In Scotland the church has aimed to have the best of both worlds with freedom to manage its own affairs but at the same time with a firm commitment to the link with the state, symbolically represented by the presence of the Queen's Commissioner at the General Assembly. More explicit than any symbolism is the statement in Chapter 23 of the Westminster Confession that:

> The civil magistrate may not assume to himself the administration of the Word and sacraments, or the power of the keys of the kingdom of heaven: yet he hath authority, and it is his duty, to take order that unity and peace be preserved in the Church, that the truth of God be kept pure and entire, that all blasphemies and heresies be suppressed, all corruptions and abuse in worship and discipline be presented or referred, and all the ordinances of God duly settled, administered and observed. For the better effecting whereof, he hath power to call synods, to be present at them and to provide that whatsoever is transacted in them be according to the mind of God.

It is significant that the proof texts quoted to support this passage cannot appeal to the New Testament except in the issue of reinforcing the role of the preachers. Their only appeal is to Old Testament references to the theocracy to buttress their claims for the ruler's role within the church. Certainly they would search in vain for any support from the New Testament, as I have attempted to show in an earlier chapter.

Some may dismiss all this as perhaps interesting for someone who enjoys historical study, but of little or no practical relevance to the present time. Let me turn such critics' attention to Northern Ireland and South Africa where the underlying religious ideas behind those two tragic situations are the very ones we have traced in the long story of post-Constantinian Christianity. It is because the Irish situation so well illustrates the sacral society, that is, the community seen as a holy people, that I describe it in fuller detail. It must, however, be remembered that the same mentality can be seen in the USA and in other parts of the world.

The first major incursion into Ireland from England came in the twelfth century when in 1172 Henry II landed with his troops. In some ways it is not quite fair to call it an English invasion since Henry was one of the successors of the Norman French kings whose forebear, William the Conqueror, had in the same way forced his way into England. The Ireland to which they came was a very different island from England in that it was Gaelic speaking and was more closely related in its ethnic roots to the Britons whom the Anglo-Saxons had forced out of England into Wales and Cornwall. This Anglo-Norman invasion only occupied part of the country and in fact it gradually shrank over the next couple of centuries until the English area comprised what was known as 'the pale', a stretch of land in the east of the country including Dublin.

The next major attempt to subjugate the whole island came with Henry VIII's decision in 1541 to proclaim himself King of Ireland and to aim at total conquest. Celtic resistance persisted though, especially in Ulster, to the end of the reign of Elizabeth when it was finally crushed. The period is of particular interest as far as the theme of this book is concerned as it marked the attempt to use the Protestant faith as a means of reinforcing the conquest.

Thus one very significant step taken by Elizabeth was the foundation in 1492 of the University of Dublin, more popularly known as Trinity College. It was modelled on the Cambridge collegiate system, but what was of more significance was the aim in view. It was to provide an educated clergy for the Anglican church in Ireland. That church was, and would continue to be, a small minority of the population. Yet it was like its sister church, the Church of England, the established church whose clergy were maintained by the reluctant peasants forced by law to pay their tithes to support what they saw as an alien clergy. From Elizabeth's point of view the clergy were to act as civilising agents imparting English culture in their parishes to a conquered population.

The situation became more complex in James I's reign with the arrival of large numbers of English and Scottish settlers in Northern Ireland. The Earl of Ulster and the Earl of Tyrconnel, two of the leaders of Celtic resistance to the English invasion, fled to France in 1605. London reacted by declaring their lands forfeit to the crown and expelling large numbers of the native Irish from their lands to make room for the incoming English settlers in what became known as the Ulster Plantation. Meanwhile other areas denuded by the fighting were also being occupied by incoming Scots. Not all the natives were excluded, for the government agents were ready to be bribed to allow them to return to their land. The result was a mixed population of English, Scots and Irish.

All three of these groups, however, had a similar religious background as far as the issue of church and nation was concerned. While the Protestant incomers were far removed in doctrine from the Catholic Irish, and while they had their own bitter divisions between Anglicans and Presbyterians, all of them maintained the same basic fallacy by identifying the church and the nations. Thus for the Irish, Ireland was and still is a Catholic land with Mary invoked as 'Queen of the Gaels'. The English came with their background of the established church, and of course that same church was now the state church in Ireland because of English conquest. The Scots who came were imbued with the notion of the kirk as being the national church in Scotland. All three groups behaved and spoke—and indeed still speak—as if their church was the embodiment of the theocratic ideal of God's church for God's nation, with God's rulers presiding over it. Lest this may seem far-fetched let me recall the famous slogan of a former Ulster prime minister that he served 'a Protestant parliament for a Protestant people'.

To return to the subsequent developments in Ireland which mirror the sacral society, we inevitably encounter the name of Oliver Cromwell. From one point of view he came as the army commander to suppress the rebellion against English rule and to punish the Irish for the massacre in 1641 of the English colonists. From the Irish point of view he was the ruthless perpetrator of the massacre of Drogheda when no one was spared and every one was put to the sword. From Cromwell's own point of view, and that of many of his supporters, he was the servant of the Lord sent to destroy the enemies of God's people, just as Joshua had destroyed the Canaanites.

The same sacralism led Bishop Jeremy Taylor in 1662 to eject the Presbyterian ministers from their parishes, just as the Puritan clergy were being ejected in England. This was modified, doubtless for reasons of state, by the payment of the Regium Donum (the Royal Gift) as an annual subsidy to the Presbyterian ministers.

Such was not the treatment accorded to Roman Catholic priests and people. Following the victory of Protestant William III over Catholic James II, the penal laws against Catholics began to be introduced. Roman Catholics were allowed to worship, but were excluded from the army, the civil service, municipal corporations and the legal profession. Roman Catholics were forbidden to send children abroad to be educated. They could not buy land from a Protestant. If they left land in their will and one son became a Protestant, he received all. If a Protestant woman married a Roman Catholic, her land went to the Protestant next of kin—and so it went on.

Today it may seem to us sheer injustice and repression. Yet, after all, the ruler was doing what the Westminster Confession required in defending what he saw to be the true faith, and penalising those he viewed as enemies of the faith. Sacralism by its very confusing of church and state inevitably leads to the employment of state repression to support church goals. Lest people in England assume that only in Scotland or Ireland are such ideas real, they should remember the laws of succession to the throne. The sovereign must be a Protestant, at least in profession, even if as in the case of someone like George IV such profession is vastly different from practice. Were the Prince of Wales to become a Roman Catholic he would be excluded from the throne. It is one of those accepted facts which conceal the underlying principle.

One of the most brilliant and penetrating analyses of the Irish situation has come from the pen of Conor Cruise O'Brien, formerly Irish government minister, United Nations emissary and editor of the *Observer*. He saw what many evangelical Christians have failed to see, namely the failure to appreciate the difference between the Old Covenant and the New Covenant. Thus in his *States of Ireland* he commented with rare discernment on the way Gaelic poetry identified the Irish nation with the Old Testament people of Israel: 'The Gaels were the children of Israel and of course "the enemies of God" were the Protestants, who were themselves the children of Israel in their own eyes. One could say that Ireland was inhabited, not really by Protestants and Catholics but by two sets of imaginary Jews.'[3]

5
The Responsible Citizen

How you behave as a citizen will clearly be deeply influenced by how you view the state of which you are a part and the government whose laws, tax demands, and customs requirements are part of everyday living. Assume that the state institution is simply the product of social evolution and you will see yourself as the arbiter of how you respond. You will thus decide if in your view any given law is a good law or a bad one, and as a result your obedience will be in terms of minimal consent where you disapprove. If, however, as a Christian you accept the biblical position that the state is divinely ordained, you will be constrained to accept government requirements as having a divinely-given authority which calls for the kind of response which you would or should give to any servant of the Lord.

This means that you begin with a frank and ready acknowledgement of the special status which the government official has—whether it is a cabinet minister or a village policeman. Admittedly these people may abuse their positions and act in an arbitrary fashion, but they are still as Paul said 'the Lord's servants' (Rom 13:4,6) and to be treated accordingly.

Paul in fact uses two Greek words which have become part of church vocabulary. The first one is seen in our word 'deacon' and the second in the term 'liturgy'. The latter word has acquired an almost entirely religious connotation, but in Paul's day it could be used not only of the one who served the Lord in the worship of the congregation, but also of the one who served the same Lord, even if unaware of his true Master, in the service of the state.

Any Christian will, or should, respect the one who serves as a deacon or leads the people to worship. There should be a like regard for the government official.

This respect for government was not some fresh or novel idea of Paul's. It was expressed by Jesus himself in his reply to the Pharisees' attempt to trick him into a compromising or seditious statement. To them the Roman emperor was head of an imperial regime which held their nation and many other people in a form of colonial subjection. To add to the normal resentment of any nationalistic Jew there was the further consideration that Caesar was a godless pagan. To a nation which looked back to God's call to Abraham and to such great Israelite kings as David, it was galling to have their capital dominated by a Roman governor and to be policed by Caesar's soldiers. If anything more was needed to fuel and itensify this resentment it was their long-cherished expectation of the coming of the Messiah who, they hoped, would sweep the Roman troops and government out of the holy land. Their resentment boiled over into bitter indignation when Jesus, whom his disciples recognised as the long-awaited Messiah, gave little or no indication of an appeal to arms to expel the foreign occupying power.

Their question: 'Is it right to pay taxes to Caesar or not?' (Mt 22:17) was thus not only a trick question, but also reflected bitter feelings. Very many Jews would probably have answered with a vigorous negative while at the same time recognising that they had little option in view of Caesar's power. Yet whether it was the forced acquiescence of the average citizen, or the resentful compliance of the Zealots, there was basically with many a refusal to acknowledge Caesar.

Now clearly Jesus would have shared their opinion as to Caesar's paganism and ungodliness. He would likewise have recognised that it was a sorry condition of things that a foreign power should occupy the city of David. At the same time he saw what they failed to see, namely the reality of divine judgement. It had happened again and again in Old Testament times when the Lord had withheld his protection from a disobedient people. The God who had destroyed Pharaoh, routed the Canaanites and scattered the Assyrian invaders, was the same eternal Judge who had opened the gates of Zion to the Babylonians and now to the Romans.

They must therefore recognise that the imperial power of Rome was the one recognised by the Lord. Indeed, as Jesus pointed out elsewhere, this same God would answer their rejection of the Messiah by granting a final and terrible sanction to Caesar to destroy the holy city and scatter the people. Hence he is quite clear—they must realise that Caesar is the ruler to whom they must submit.

At the same time as he replied to their impatient nationalism he completely exploded their attempt to trick him by pointing to their own lack of consistency. Thus in asking them to show him a Roman denarius with its imperial image he was reminding them that they had come to terms with Roman currency. Indeed some of them had come to terms with it to very profitable effect. To use the currency of the realm is to acknowledge the government which is the ultimate guarantor of that currency and so of ordinary economic existence. Consistency demands that such recognition should face the practical consequence in a readiness to comply with government demands.

The apostle Peter followed the same line of teaching when he urged believers to 'honour the king' (1 Pet 2:17). By the time Peter wrote, the feelings of resentment must have been greatly accentuated. It was bad enough to have to acknowledge an emperor like Augustus who at least preserved peace and social stability. When, however, you had a blackguard like Nero how could you possibly honour him? The cynical occupant of the imperial throne had scant regard for anyone but himself. The city of Rome was there for his profit, and a helpless minority like the Christians could provide a useful diversion if their bloody torture would deflect public attention from his own misdeeds. Yet Peter is as unwavering in his attitude as were his Master and his colleague, Paul. We are to reverence the office of the ruler even if the man who occupies it disgraces the regime by his own excesses.

In a modern democracy there can be deep cleavage within the

nation. The current government may be deeply resented by an electorate which hopes to use the ballot box to remove them. Such feelings of opposition are perfectly legitimate, but they must not, for the Christian, degenerate into the scurrilous abuse or cynical insult which too often emerge as the voice of opposition. The present government is there by divine providence and we must accord the respect which is due to their position. If the early Christians could accord respect to the rule of a ruthless tyrant like Nero then surely we must be ready to give honour to those who rule us.

Mention of the ballot box as the way to remove a government within the framework of law is a reminder that in many countries this opportunity does not exist. The disenfranchised black population of South Africa has been deprived of its basic democratic right, even though it constitutes the overwhelming majority of the population. Across the world, in dictatorships both of the left and of the right, there are people in a similar plight. They live under governments which they did not elect and would not willingly have elected. There are no non-violent means by which they can change the political system under which they suffer. Are they then simply to endure with passive stolidity, or are they to listen to those who urge revolutionary violence as the only way of toppling tyrants from power? More insistently, the question comes to Christians—should they not be prepared to throw in their lot with those involved in the revolutionary struggle?

To many readers this may seem a theoretical issue to which a simplistic answer may at once be given, that the Christian may never engage in such subversive action. It certainly was not a theoretical issue when the miners' strike of 1984 exploded into violence and pickets fought and were scattered by mounted police. It was the same issue in the bitter dispute when the *Times* and the *Sun* newspapers were moved to Wapping. The printers, like the miners, felt that a ruthless boss was backed by a sympathetic government using laws designed to break the power of the trade unions. In both cases violence was the outcome, with the police caught in the middle. For a Christian miner or printer the struggle for jobs was a struggle for economic survival. The issue of acknowledging the government was a painful matter of conscience.

It is a still more practical issue for black Christians in South Africa who see family life destroyed by a professedly Christian government which, by the economic trap of migrant labour, keeps miners herded in a male society while their wives and children are far away in the enforced exile of life in so-called homelands. It is also an agonising matter of conscience for young white Christian men in South Africa facing conscription into the army to suppress the black townships or refusing and facing a prison sentence.

It is similarly no theoretical issue in parts of Latin America where the voice of protest is silenced in the torture rooms and the death-dealing prisons of totalitarian governments. When the Christian sees the exploiters fabulously wealthy, while the poor are reduced to a squalor and poverty which strips them of ordinary human dignity, can he remain silent? Must he remain inactive? Is there no place for direct action?

If some Christians make an appeal to the Old Testament to justify the establishment of a national church, may other Christians not make the same appeal to justify armed struggle? If the Westminster Confession can appeal to the Old Testament to justify granting to the ruler the responsibility to restrain heretics, may other Christians not follow the same line of reasoning? After all, Jehu was anointed by the prophet Elisha and given the mandate from the Lord to topple the evil regime of Ahab.

It is not surprising therefore that the anguish of those who see the grievous exploitation of the poor in many Latin American countries has given birth to what has been called liberation theology. The radicals who embrace this teaching—and surely one must acknowledge the ugliness of the regimes which have driven them down this line—are expressing their own deep moral revulsion at cruelty, and their deep pity for the suffering poor. At the same time they are trying to formulate a biblical statement of doctrine which will both explain their actions and vindicate them.

Christ is thus seen as the great liberator who sets men free. He is seen as the One who obviously championed the cause of the poor. His stern denunciation of ill-gotten wealth, and of the men who exploited others, is justifiably quoted. His scattering of the money-changers from the Temple courts is cited. His scathing indictment of those who robbed the widows and covered their evil deeds with a cloak of piety is heard again in a context where too often churches have apparently seen their role as the sanctifying of the status quo.

Such radicals will point to the biblical stress on justice and ask if there could be more forthright denunciations of greed and exploitation than the words of Amos or Hosea. They will also point to the strong biblical emphasis in both Old and New Testaments on compassion for the weak. The Law of Moses made special provision for the widow, the fatherless and the foreigner. There was the Law of the Jubilee which insisted on the return of land to those who had been forced by poverty or debt to sell it to their richer countrymen. There was a prohibition against gathering every last piece of harvest, or gleaning every olive or grape, since provision must be made for the poor and needy.

While one may sympathise with the liberation theologian in his cry for justice for the oppressed, one must still examine his arguments in the light of Scripture, beginning with the most basic issue of all, the nature of God. The God who is revealed in the Bible is the transcendent One who is above and beyond his creation. True, he is deeply involved in his dealings with men within the creation. Yet always he is viewed as the reigning Lord. Too much current thinking, even what is claimed to be Christian thinking, is shot through with pantheism, that is with the notion that God is everything and everything is God. Thus there is no clear distinction between Creator and creation. God is part of, or perhaps it would be more correct to say the sum total of, everything. Thus God is in a state of development, and the evolutionary development of the world and the human conflicts which move towards peace and justice, are all part of the development of God.

The God of the Bible is, however, Lord over all things and over all men. Isaiah gives a marvellous glimpse of the transcendence of our God: 'He sits enthroned above the circle of the earth, and its people are like grasshoppers. He stretches out the heavens like a canopy, and spreads them out like a tent to live in. He brings princes to naught and reduces the rulers of this world to nothing' (Is 40: 22–23).

This transcendent God is, however, not only the Judge of the rulers, he is also the Judge of the revolutionaries. Just as he may utilise godless rulers, so he may utilise equally godless rebels to be the rod of his anger against injustice, and the ministers of his judgement. Yet this neither justifies the rebel in his actions, nor makes him immune from judgement on his own behaviour. Thus while Jehu's rebellion against Ahab was an administration of divine justice, his own evil, and that of his successors, led to God's judgement on the line of Jehu, when his great grandson was assassinated in a coup similar to the one by which God removed Ahab.

Allied to this failure to see God as the supreme Judge over both repressive ruler and liberating revolutionary, is the further failure to recognise the true nature of man. The optimistic assumption is constantly made that if only men and women could be liberated from oppression and poverty, a new day would dawn. This, however, fails to take into account the fall of man so graphically presented in Genesis 3. The image of God which made man a reflection of his Creator has been sadly defaced. Men and women are sinners and that means inherently selfish. It is not surprising therefore that yesterday's poor can become tomorrow's ruthless exploiters, and yesterday's oppressed can become tomorrow's oppressors.

With this dual failure to recognise the true glory of God and the true nature of man, there is a consequent failure to appreciate that what is primarily needed for rich and poor, ruler and governed, is reconciliation to God. It is only reconciled sinners who have the Holy Spirit of truth and love dwelling within them, who will be able to begin, even if rather slowly and painfully, to become reconciled to each other.

It is interesting to contrast the development of the French Revolution of 1789 with the spiritual revolution wrought by the evangelical revival in England. The revolution in France produced a blood bath which consumed its own leaders in the reign of terror, and led to the reaction of the military dictatorship of Napoleon, who plunged most of Europe into war. The revival preachers in England saw not only thousands of the semi-slaves of the industrial revolution converted, but also some from the ruling classes as well. The results were the social changes which finally swept away the slave trade, ameliorated the hideous conditions in factories, raised the status of women and set children free, while at the same time producing a trade union movement whose inspiration was the social conscience of the great awakening.

The Exodus has been widely used—or indeed misused—to justify the struggle of the oppressed to break the chains of their slavery. What is forgotten is that it was not some slave revolt which set Israel free, but the direct and miraculous intervention of the Almighty. The call 'let my people go' was not the defiant response of a rebel leader. Rather it was the command of God which Pharaoh rejected with catastrophic consequences, both for him and for his people. Furthermore, the story of the Exodus is used in the New Testament, not as a blue print for rebellion, but as the picture of the even greater deliverance when sinners are rescued 'from the dominion of darkness and brought . . . into the kingdom of the Son he loves' (Col 1:13).

A further truth ignored by those who try to ally gospel and revolution is the biblical stress on eternity. While the kingdom of God is already here in the lives of God's people, it is not yet *fully* here in that its final manifestation of peace, justice and happiness has not yet come. The radical attempt to realise the final kingdom here and now is doomed to failure. Such attempts always have failed and always will fail until the perfect conditions of a new heaven and a new earth make social harmony complete.

The jibe often repeated by Marxists, that religion is the opiate of the masses, can be answered not only by the appeal to Scripture, but by the evidence of experience and of history. The Marxist revolution did not produce the brotherhood of the classless society. It led rather to years of wholesale slaughter, of grim prison camps, of perverted psychiatric torture. It led to the elitism of the party faithful, with their special privileges. It produced the social stagnation and the enormous economic decline which with many other sad results have loaded communist leaders with massive problems to solve.

This is by no stretch of the imagination a plea for a swing to the political right. Human sinfulness and corruption are as evident in right wing governments as in left wing ones. The greed, covetousness and callous ambition of the unrestrained market place simply presents another angle on human selfishness.

It is significant that when the true liberation of men and women takes place, it has a far more deep-seated and lasting effect. The Christian slaves of the Roman empire might still be viewed as chattels to be abused by ruthless masters, but they had acquired a dignity which no one could take from them. It is also significant that those who have been most heavenly minded have been the very men and women who have worked with determined zeal and tireless persistence for social change.

The Tolpuddle Martyrs, founders of the first farm workers' trade union and deported to the convict colony in Australia for so doing, were in the first place Methodists and local preachers. At the other end of the social scale in nineteenth-century England, Lord Shaftesbury was unflagging in his zeal for home missions, yet left an abiding memory as one of the great social reformers—no wonder the poor of London lined the streets for his funeral!

The main thesis of this chapter has been that the Christian is called upon to acknowledge the dignity of the ruler even if the representative of government is far from being what he ought to be. This, however, is no traditionalist clinging to the established order. Nor is it a blind indifference to the pains and sufferings of the oppressed. Rather it is an awareness that God sets up rulers and can and does remove them. It is a realisation that sinful men and women need more than social improvement—important though that is. They need new life in Christ and a solid hope which reaches beyond the grave. Finally, it is an acknowledgement that the state is the instrument to control wickedness and promote social benefits, and while the government of the day may grievously fail in its mission, it is yet set there by God and should therefore be respected.

This issue of respect for government and refusal to use illegitimate means of opposition is seen in the Northern Ireland situation. On both sides of the struggle there are those who appeal not only to the ballot box but to the bullet. The para-military is too often the adjunct to the political front. Tragically even Christians have succumbed to this. One recalls the sorry event of an evangelical minister parading followers rather ostentatiously brandishing firearms certificates. The fact that they were designated a third force indicates that they were not showing the certificates to indicate that they held weapons legally to shoot rabbits!

To such, and indeed to any other manifestation across the world where vigilantes take the law into their own hands, and lynch law prevails, one must reply with the attitude and words of Jesus. His attitude was seen in his refusal to respond to the popular clamour to be recognised by the excited crowd as their King. It was also seen in his inclusion of Simon the Zealot in his band of disciples. To take a one-time para-military activist and to teach him that the new kingdom was to be enlarged by spiritual and peaceful means only, was to make a public declaration that subversion had no place in the life of the Christian. To place that same Zealot in a situation where in following his Master he must respect the Caesar whom he had formerly detested and tried to oppose by violence—this was to remind him and us that respect for a government, even one of which we could not approve, is nonetheless a plain Christian responsibility.

When Jesus himself was personally involved in his trial before Pilate, he demonstrated that the requirement to recognise the governing authorities was not only part of his teaching, but was his own attitude. Thus he was ready to submit to the Roman judicial process. This did not mean an abject submission. So he was quite prepared to remind his judge that the latter's authority was derived from God: 'You would have no power over me if it were not given to you from above' (Jn 19:11). Yet while in no way abating his claims and while making a firm defence, he nonetheless submitted to Pilate. The latter might out of cowardice capitulate to pressure and perpetuate an injustice, but he was the emperor's representative and therefore the judicial office was to be respected, even if the occupant was tarnishing that office by his own craven failure.

Jesus was consistent in this attitude of respect for authority which of necessity precluded an appeal to any other means to achieve desired goals. Violence was ruled out since the kingdom where love reigned could not without gross contradiction be maintained or enlarged by force. His disciples were firmly reminded of the break with the pattern of Israel's life in the period of the Old Testament. It was with this in mind that they appealed to the precedent of the prophet's judgement on Ahaziah's soldiers (2 Kings 1:10) and asked in face of an unwelcoming Samaritan village: 'Lord, do you want us to call fire down from heaven to destroy them?' (Lk 9:54). The reply was a firm rebuke, which was echoed in an equally stern word to Peter in Gethsemane when he tried to defend his Master with the sword: 'Put your sword back in its place . . . for all who draw the sword will die by the sword. Do you think I cannot call on my Father, and he will at once put at my disposal more than twelve legions of angels?' (Mt 26: 52–53).

When he stood before Pilate, the Prince of Peace had the same message of non-violence: 'My kingdom is not of this world. If it were, my servants would fight to prevent my arrest by the Jews. But now my kingdom is from another place' (Jn 18:36). Could there be a more emphatic rejection of the idea that Christians may ever resort to violence—even in the noblest cause?

The apostle Paul fully acknowledged the right of the government to 'bear the sword' (Rom 13:4) and thus to employ force to reinforce the law. Yet he is equally clear that the Christian has no mandate to make the same appeal. 'For though we live in the world, we do not wage war as the world does. The weapons we fight with are not the weapons of the world. On the contrary, they have divine power to demolish strongholds' (2 Cor 10:3–4). When he gives the vivid picture of the Christian soldier, the offensive weapon is 'the sword of the spirit, which is the word of God' (Eph 6:17). It is the paradox of true Christian liberation theology that when the church is most defenceless 'we are more than conquerors through him who loved us' (Rom 8:37).

6

Limits to Obedience

The last chapter emphasised respect for government and queried the advocacy of subversion, even in a good cause. This, however, prompts further important questions: What is involved in being law-abiding? Are there no limits to the submission we give to the state, or if there is a limit, how do we refuse to comply with the law without infringing the basic principle of respect for the divinely-authorised organs of government?

The limit to our obedience is well indicated by the apostles' response to their interrogators who were insisting that they stop preaching. Their reply was simple but far-reaching in its implications: 'We must obey God rather than men!' (Acts 5:29). Since the state is by God's ordaining, our obedience to the laws of the state is obedience to God, but when the ruling powers step beyond their mandate and make demands which are contrary to God's revealed truth, then the Christian conscience is compelled to say 'No'.

That refusal will only come in face of serious provocation to violate conscience and disobey God's will. Since this is out of the question, the believer has to withhold obedience, but only on this issue. It does not give any excuse whatsoever for wholesale refusal to obey. In other words, we go as far as we can down the road of obedience and even when compelled by conscience to disobey, we still aim to maintain in every other area full submission to the legitimate requirements of the law.

Someone may object that this is to revert to the kind of subjective attitude which earlier I rejected. Is this not, the objector asks, simply a return to the claim that I obey the laws which I approve and disobey the ones I disapprove? In fact it is not a reversion to that position at all. Rather it is an acknowledgement that while general obedience is the norm, there can come an extreme situation when an intolerable demand is made. So it is not a case of picking and choosing according to my own fancy. Rather it is being driven into a corner by a government which has stepped right outside its domain. What is at issue is the kind of requirement which no Christian could possibly accept without denying the even greater authority of the Sovereign God to whose judgement both governors and governed are ultimately subject.

Before considering how to handle the abnormal situation where conscience requires non-compliance, it would be best to examine the normal situation in which law-abiding should be the glad and willing reaction. Earlier we saw how Jesus exemplified the response to the state by his willing submission to the Roman authorities, and by his clear endorsement of the responsibility of those who utilised the national currency to obey the government which sustained that currency. We will find the same consistency with Paul who, as we saw in a much earlier chapter, insisted on the divine origin of state authority. Like his Master, he not only spelled out the nature of this obedience, but illustrated it in his own attitude and actions.

Paul was by birth a Jew, but he was also a Roman citizen and he was profoundly thankful for both these privileges. Indeed he was ready to appeal to that citizenship to experience the protection of the law against unjust attacks by his own people. So too when he was brought before the Roman governors, Felix and Festus, he argued vigorously for the legality of his own conduct. His very argument was an indication that he saw himself as subject to the law of the empire and so to the judges who were appointed to maintain it.

The contention that he was a loyal and law-abiding citizen was endorsed again and again by Roman officials. Luke, the author of the Acts, clearly had in mind the constant charges that Christians were subversives and a danger to society. His record of Paul's various encounters with Roman officialdom was a firm rebuttal of such charges. Gallio in Achaia brushed aside the obviously false accusations of the Jewish leaders. Claudius Lysias in Jerusalem protected him from the Jewish mob and sent him under armed escort to the governor with the frank admission that as far as he could see 'there was no charge against him that deserved death or imprisonment' (Acts 23:29). Festus, the governor, came to the same conclusion. Paul had given his final endorsement of government authority by appealing to the supreme judicial court, that of the emperor, and Festus had to admit that it really was 'unreasonable to send on a prisoner without specifying the charges against him' (Acts 25:27).

Paul's teaching is thus the reflection of his personal attitude. His own submission to the authorities is seen in his requirement that Christians should be subject not only to the emperor but to the officials of the empire. This was a particularly needful word for the people of Crete who were restive under Roman rule; hence his firm reminder to them 'to be subject to rulers and authorities, to be obedient, to be ready to do whatever is good' (Tit 3:1).

There are incentives in this matter of obedience. The first and basic one is fear. If you break the law you will face the consequences. To fallen man, it is often the fear of detection, and the knowledge of the painful results of detection, which deter the wrongdoer. For Paul, however, there is a deeper reason in that the representative of the law is a servant of God, even if he himself does not recognise that fact, and so is 'an agent of wrath' (Rom 13:4).

In the context it seems clearly to be the wrath of God which is displayed in the actions of the police, the courts and the prisons. The ungodly may dismiss this, but the Christian will take it very seriously, remembering that while reconciled to God and having free access into his presence it is still the King of kings to whom we come. It is the letter to Hebrews which stresses the boldness of our approach yet also reminds us that 'our God is a consuming fire' (Heb 12:29).

Paul adds a further stimulus to the obedience which is to be yielded. 'It is necessary to submit to the authorities, not only because of possible punishment but also because of conscience' (Rom 13:5). The person in the world may keep within the law simply because he is afraid of being detected. The Christian must obey because he has been summoned to holiness. Having responded to God's call, 'Be holy, because I am holy' (1 Pet 1:16), he has a stronger incentive to law-abiding than the fear of detection. Hence he does not drive within the speed limit because he sees a police car in his mirror, but because his conscience tells him to. He does not refrain from smuggling only because he has heard that customs officers are being specially alert.

Peter makes this particular incentive even more explicit when he insists: 'Submit yourselves for the Lord's sake to every authority instituted among men: whether to the king, as the supreme authority, or to governors, who are sent by him to punish those who do wrong and to commend those who do right' (1 Pet 2:13–14). There is a dual significance in this command. On the one hand it stresses what we have seen is constantly emphasised in the New Testament, that because it is the Lord who has ordained the state, we obey the authorities in order to obey God.

There is also a further related factor. As Christians we are the known representatives of the living God. Our failures will be a bad testimony and give opportunity to ungodly people to dismiss the gospel. On the other side, our righteous living seen in honest and law-abiding practice, will be a positive aid to evangelism. 'It is God's will,' says Peter, 'that by doing good you should silence the ignorant talk of foolish men' (1 Pet 2:15).

All this has implications as far as taxation is concerned. Few people relish paying tax and many will use any device to avoid it. Indeed tax dodgers have become a substantial group within the nation, and tax evasion is often viewed not as a criminal offence but as a natural human attempt to escape a most unwelcome imposition. Paul will have none of this. The authorities, he insists, are God's servants—the word is literally 'deacons'—with a full right to issue tax demands.

He enumerates two main areas of taxation—tax on the person,

and revenue which covers the various levies on property and trade, whether import duties or excise charges. The idea of fiddling tax returns should be anathema. So too would be any dabbling in the so-called black economy. It even rules out totally the petty smuggling in which some Christians engage as they return from holidays abroad, and which they seem to think is a bit of a joke. It is not something to report to friends with some measure of pride, but rather something of which to repent with shame before God.

This brings us to the major issue of disobedience for conscience sake. Indeed all that has preceded must make the problem of possible disobedience all the more complex. In view of this overwhelming emphasis on the authority of the state and our responsibility to obey, it becomes all the more difficult to know when we must refuse, and perhaps even more difficult to decide how that refusal is to be carried out.

In the first place it must be very strongly stated that reaching the limit has nothing to do with personal likes or dislikes. Furthermore it has nothing to do with possible reactions to an unreasonable, unjust or even repressive exercise of state power. The Christians who received Peter's first letter faced that kind of situation. Immorality, injustice and cruelty were on the imperial throne. Christians were facing an increasing wave of bloody persecution. It would have been all too easy to argue that they did not owe anything to a government which treated them with injustice and callous brutality. Yet it was to these very Christians that Peter sent his firm commands to submit which we discussed earlier in this chapter.

It is not only in the area of citizenship that it is difficult to detect when we are facing an issue of conscience and when we are being influenced by other considerations. Unless we have learned to check our own temperament, and to guard against our own individual foibles, we will be liable to set the conscience boundary in an arbitrary fashion. We may claim to be governed by principle, but sadly what is claimed to be principle can often be seen by an impartial onlooker as prejudice or sheer pig-headed obstinacy. There is also such a thing as the martyr complex, where people seem to relish being the victim and cannot always see that their plight may be partly of their own making. I recall an acid comment on King Charles I that he was not the victim of disloyal men, nor was he suffering for righteous principles, but was rather a martyr to his own stupidity! So we need to walk warily at this point.

The limit is only reached when, as we honestly follow biblical principles and as we examine our own hearts before God, we still find ourselves confronted by a clear conflict between our duty to God and our duty to the state. However, Christians differ in matters of conscience, as Paul so well demonstrates in the discussion in Romans 14. Different believers may set the limit of obedience at different points. We must then avoid the two extremes to which Paul refers in that chapter—on one side censuring our brother, and on the other despising him. Both censure and scorn are ruled out since each of us must stand before God, and for each of us it is equally true: 'To his own master he stands or falls' (Rom 14:4).

Making allowance for this freedom in personal judgement, we must surely all agree that the limit of obedience is reached when we are commanded to do what is plainly contrary to God's truth, or when forbidden to do what is plainly commanded by the Lord. Jesus himself made clear that the limit is reached when God's will is challenged. Thus, while firmly endorsing the sovereignty of government with his: 'Give to Caesar what is Caesar's,' he equally firmly endorsed the supreme sovereignty of heaven, as he added the vitally important qualifying words 'and to God what is God's.' Caesar has a right to demand loyal obedience from the citizens, Christians included, but only God has the right to demand total and unqualified obedience. Where Caesar's demands clash with God's, there is no question as to which authority is supreme and which demand must be obeyed, whatever the cost.

The early believers in the Roman empire found that breaking point when they were commanded to offer a pinch of incense at the shrine of the emperor. No one, they replied, could at one and the same time say 'Caesar is Lord' and 'Jesus is Lord'. Similarly, when Christians in the Soviet Union were forbidden to teach their children and young people the gospel, they felt they would be in flagrant defiance of God's word if they were to comply with the state's edict.

John Calvin, the great Reformer of the sixteenth century, wrote with sharp insight on this issue:

> But in that obedience which we hold to be due to the commands of rulers, we must always make the exception, nay, must be particularly careful that it is not incompatible with obedience to him to whose will the works of all kings should be subject, to whose decrees their commands must yield, to whose majesty their sceptres must bow. And, indeed, how preposterous were it, in pleasing men to incure the offence of him for whose sake you obey men! The Lord, therefore, is King of kings. When he opens his sacred mouth, he alone is to be heard, instead of all and above all. We are subject to the men who rule over us but subject only in the Lord. If they command anything against him let us not pay the least regard to it, nor be moved by all the dignity which they possess as magistrates—a dignity to which no injury is done when it is subordinated to the special and truly supreme power of God.[4]

The problem can be aggravated during civil war which may last for a considerable time and produce a situation where it is difficult to decide which is the legitimate authority. This was so in seventeenth-century England. In that situation it was not a revolt by dissident subject against the ruler. It was more complex in that it was a constitutional clash between two recognised centres of authority in the state, namely king and parliament. It was somewhat similar in the American civil war, where the battle was ultimately between the leaders of the southern states and the northern ones, in which the issue was where final sovereignty lay.

In such situations, and indeed in the more frequent context of armed revolt or military coup, the Christian will face complex and painful problems. This was so when the dictator Marcos was overthrown in the Philippines. Many church leaders considered they were justified in leading their people to side with what became a popular uprising against tyranny. In the confusion of such a time, and in the blurring of issues by the propaganda which pours out from both sides, it is not easy to reach a conclusion. Truth in times of conflict is usually one of the early casualties. What then is the Christian to do?

Governed as he must be by his basic principles, he will be reluctant to side with what is clearly a rebellion. He will be compelled by conscience to yield obedience to the existing government until it is clear that the authority has passed to new hands and the claims of the older regime are clearly no longer linked to the reality of the situation.

Some may suggest that that savours of lack of principle. Is it not simply going with the crowd and endorsing for convenience or comfort's sake rather than for conscience sake what happens to be the established position? It is in fact neither since the Christian may have few grounds for respecting the integrity or the moral standards either of the deposed or of the rebels. It is rather that he sees behind the sound and fury of men and behind human greed and ambition, the overruling providence of God who raises up and sets down. 'No-one from the east or the west or from the desert can exalt a man. But it is God who judges: He brings one down, he exalts another' (Ps 75:6–7).

It is important, however, to qualify the whole idea of disobedience. Such can be either active or passive. The former I have argued is ruled out as far as the Christian is concerned. Neither subversion nor acts of civil disobedience are options. Not only does the call to obedience in the Scriptures reject any appeal to violence, or any attempt to subvert or overthrow a government by force, it also rejects such acts of civil disobedience as disrupting car or rail traffic by sitting on roads or platform. It also rules out refusal to pay taxes or to fill in either an electoral roll or a census form.

This does not mean a total absence of any sign of disobedience. The passive withholding of obedience involves not only a refusal to obey a command which clearly violates Christian conscience, but also a readiness to suffer the consequences. The Christians in the Roman empire remained loyal citizens even when they refused the idolatrous worship of the emperor. They were ready to face the consequences which meant torture and even death.

Yet it was this passive disobedience which was to prove such a powerful weapon. It was their patient suffering which proved to be the anvil on which the sword of persecution was finally blunted.

There is one weapon which is hidden as far as the world is concerned, but which has proved more powerful than either the greatest regimes or the most radical revolutionary forces. That secret weapon is prayer. Here the Christian, though apparently crushed by irresistible brute force, has recourse to an even greater power—the omnipotence of God. The Christian does not turn to prayer as a last resort. It is not an attempt to buoy up one's spirits in an otherwise intolerable situation. It is not human despair turning inwards and using a kind of spiritual optimism or wishful thinking to find some respite. Rather it is the appeal to a power which is invincible and to a wisdom which knows both the ultimate goal of history and the best means to achieve that goal.

The non-Christian may smile at what he can only see at best as naivety and at worst as escapist superstition. The Christian by contrast has a Bible in which God has recorded for our encouragement the great stories of how prayer has proved a powerful weapon. So we go back to Exodus and see a helpless people exploited by a powerful state, absolutely unable to break its power, and with no allies to turn to for help. In their hopelessness they cried to God and it was no vain exercise. God's response was clearly stated to Moses: 'The cry of the Israelites has reached me, and I have seen the way the Egyptians are oppressing them' (Exod 3:9). It was this response from heaven to the cry of God's people which sounded the death knell of Pharaoh's tyranny.

This is a recurring pattern. In the days of the judges, and later of the kings, there are times of foreign domination and internal tyranny. Again and again the faithful remnant have no one to turn to but the Lord, and again and again the Lord acts. He may raise up someone like Jehu to topple an evil regime. He may employ one pagan nation to distract another so that Sennacherib was compelled to withdraw from Jerusalem because he feared an impending attack from Egypt. This fear was compounded by direct angelic intervention. God may even utilise domestic feuds

LIMITS TO OBEDIENCE 61

in a nation to end an evil regime. So that same Sennacherib, the scourge of Israel, was murdered by his own sons (2 Kings 19:9,35,37).

This contrast between human weakness which turns to prayer and divine omnipotence which comes to the rescue is seen in one of its most vivid forms in the restoration of Israel after the exile. The utter wretchedness and hopelessness of the people are echoed with great pathos in the psalmist's cry of anguish: 'By the rivers of Babylon we sat and wept when we remembered Zion' (Ps 137:1). The misery was compounded by the arrogance of the Babylonian victors: 'There our captors asked us for songs, our tormentors demanded songs of joy; they said, "Sing us one of the songs of Zion"' (v 3). It would have been sacrilege to respond to that taunting request. Far better surely to do as the singer did and turn to the Lord. That cry of wretchedness was, however, no escape from present misery to the temporary solace of a religious refuge. It was in fact the summons to a display of power which would finally deliver these exiles.

So in Belshazzar's palace, when it seemed as if ungodly arrogance knew no bounds and feared no foe, God intervened. The writing on the wall which sobered the king and his drunken guests was the message of God. That night the Persian army moved into the city and Babylon's sun suddenly set. In the new day of Persian domination God used the statesmanship of Cyrus as he sought to control such a diverse empire. So the edict was issued which saw the exiles returning as Isaiah had prophesied they would: 'The ransomed of the Lord will return. They will enter Zion with singing; everlasting joy will crown their heads' (Is 51:11). It seems a far cry from the wretchedness and tears of the psalmist. It was in fact the response of God to the psalmist's prayer.

The same pattern has been seen down the centuries of Christian history. When the dark night of terror and superstition hung heavily over Europe in the Middle Ages, and when the tyranny of popes and emperors seemed absolute and the tortures and deaths of believers seemed unending, God was preparing to work. The far off battles in Asia Minor might seem remote to

Christians crying to God for deliverance. Yet it was the fall of Constantinople to the Turks in 1453 which drove the scholars to the West and brought a revival of learning, which in turn led to a return to the Greek testament which was finally to liberate people and nations from tyranny, both secular and ecclesiastical.

Our own generation has seen similar happenings in various lands. Take China, for example. When Chairman Mao let loose the fanaticism of the red guards, it seemed like doom to the churches across that great land. With pastors in prison, church buildings closed, Bibles destroyed and worship forbidden (unless within sanctioned circles), it seemed like the end. Yet God's people prayed across the world and God worked. The 'gang of four' failed to perpetuate Mao's tyranny. His widow was to spend her future years in prison. Pastors were to emerge from years in prison to find the numbers of Christians multiplied vastly. Who is to say prayer is not a very powerful weapon—far more powerful than any revolutionary scheme?

So we go back to the New Testament to find strong emphases on prayer for those in authority. Such prayer is by no means an emergency mechanism in times of crisis or of persecution. It is rather to be the regular experience of the people of God. To illustrate again from the Old Testament: Nehemiah was able to respond to a sudden crisis with immediate prayer to God because he was already accustomed to spending time daily with God. It was the regular pattern of his prayer life which prepared him for the sudden demand. So Paul writes to Timothy to urge the Christians under his care to pray regularly for the government.

This call to prayer is presented as a matter of priority and of great importance. 'I urge, then' (1 Tim 2:1)—thus Paul introduces the matter. Here is an implicit acknowledgement that this is an area where Christians may be slack. It is also an insistent reminder that he is not looking for a formal response. Prayer for the government can so easily be a token intercession, formally observed in Sunday worship. This perfunctory praying—if indeed it can even be called prayer—is far from the apostle's mind. So he ranges over the whole area of the ministry of prayer to stress how comprehensive such praying should be. 'Requests, prayers, intercession and thanksgiving'—all these are included in praying for those in government. Even as I write this I am rebuked to realise how often my praying in this particular area falls so far short. I fear I speak for many others!

Paul also speaks of what we should have in view as we pray. It is 'that we may live peaceful and quiet lives in all godliness and holiness' (v 2). He knows only too well from experience how much he benefited from peaceful conditions on his preaching tours. He was thankful for the protecting might of the Roman troops who kept that peace. Hence his prayer and urging of others to pray for the government were an essential part of his praying for the work of the gospel. Those who recall the chaos and turmoil of what was then the Belgian Congo after the colonial power had withdrawn, will appreciate the importance of stable conditions for gospel work.

There is a further factor which has a strong bearing on the missionary task. There are lands which are closed firmly to the messengers of Christ. It is only God who will open those closed doors. So the Christian recalls the voice from heaven recorded in the Revelation: 'What he opens, no-one can shut; and what he shuts, no-one can open' (3:7), and hears that voice as a summons to prayer for rulers who try to shut out the gospel.

Clearly this means that such praying is not limited to one's own nation. The Christian ought to have wide horizons. The fellowship of the people of God stretches around the world. Thus, while the believer obviously has a primary responsibility to pray for his own government, his prayer must not end there. So he reads his newspaper and listens to radio or TV news, not simply to keep up to date with international affairs, but in order to translate into prayer known situations overseas with their implications for Christian worship and witness.

Paul has a further purpose in view. He does not see the saving purposes of God limited only to one stratum of society. Thus, as he urges Timothy to encourage Christians to pray for kings and all in authority, he adds the reminder that we come to 'God our Saviour who wants all men to be saved and to come to a knowledge of the truth' (1 Tim 2:3–4). Clearly we are to pray for conversions in court as well as in the market place; in government circles as well as among the poor.

When the government is tyrannical and even when it persecutes the churches, prayer is still to be focused on those in authority. Did not Jesus urge his disciples and all of us to 'pray for those who persecute you' (Mt 5:44)? I remember listening to Joseph Tonn recalling his grim but glorious days under arrest in Rumania, cross questioned but assuring his interrogator that he prayed for him. It was no wonder that the man who represented such repressive power could acknowledge before the pastor's release that he would miss him!

When the persecution waxes even hotter, and when the tyranny seems to defy heaven, there is still a confident recourse to prayer. In the final book of the Bible there is on the one side the harsh pictures of authorities trying to crush the church of Jesus, and on the other side the confidence of the saints at prayer. Indeed the praying people of God are not confined to those on earth. Those who have already suffered and died for their testimony are seen in heaven and they are still praying: 'I saw under the altar the souls of those who had been slain because of the word of God and the testimony they had maintained. They called out in a loud voice, "How long, Sovereign Lord, holy and true, until you judge the inhabitants of the earth and avenge our blood?"' (Rev 6:9–10). That glimpse of heaven should be a stimulus to us to give ourselves to prayer that God would vindicate his people and would work so powerfully among the rulers of the nations as to anticipate the final glory. That vision is clearly stated: 'The kingdom of the world has become the kingdom of our Lord and of his Christ, and he will reign for ever and ever' (Rev 11:15).

7

Party Politics

For which party should I vote at the next election? Which candidate should have my vote? These are closely allied questions, but as we shall see they are really distinct, for I may vote for a particular candidate from a party which is not my personal preference, but who has special qualities. However, before we get to this point there is a more basic issue for the Christian—to vote or not to vote at all, that is the question!

It is good to pause and reflect that while this is an issue which should be faced, it is for many Christians in the world, possibly even a majority, an interesting but utterly academic matter since whatever conclusion they reach they are not in a position to cast their votes. It is salutary for Christians who debate this matter to remember that the very debate is a luxury denied to great numbers of their fellow believers. To those who live in totalitarian regimes the question does not arise since no freedom of choice is permitted. Even for those who live in many countries which lay claim to the title 'democratic', the electorate may be so restricted, or the electoral system so corrupt, or the voting so manipulated, that again the matter of casting a vote is not really a very meaningful issue.

For those who live in true and functioning democracies, the issue of voting becomes a real one. It is an area where Christians have to learn to disagree since there are those, though probably a minority, who refuse on principle to vote. Their argument is that the Christian belongs to a heavenly kingdom and in addition is called to be separate from this world which is, according to the

New Testament, in darkness because it is under the control of the ruler of this world, namely the devil. To vote would be for such Christians a compromise with the rulers of this world.

There is with some exponents of this view a strange inconsistency, since they are not only prepared to be employed by the state, but may even make a career in the civil service, reaching the top level. When the actual government of a country is examined, it will be seen how vital the role of the civil servant is. The ministers who form the cabinet team may move from one post to another. They will have their basic political principles, but in order to implement them they will rely heavily on their civil servants to produce the statistics, the information, and indeed the draft legislation which will be presented to parliament. To be a civil servant is indeed to be far more deeply involved in government than the average citizen. It is extremely difficult to see how a Christian in such a position can refuse to vote.

In my native Ulster there is a cynical slogan: 'Vote early and vote often.' It refers to misusing the unused votes of others. The recent obituary lists are scanned to discover the names of those whose votes will obviously be unused. Likewise, those belonging to a particular denominational group will have their votes used without either their permission or even their knowledge. This, however, can hardly be used as an argument against the non-voters, as they will justifiably maintain that they cannot be held responsible for other people's misdeeds. Much more solidly biblical arguments are needed as we examine this issue.

In the first place we must scrutinise more closely the whole idea of 'separation'. It is certainly true that separation is taught in the New Testament, but it can hardly be construed as total abstinence from the entire political process. With the background of the Old Testament ceremonial laws, it is clear that separation relates to that which is unclean in God's sight. If, however, the state is divinely ordained, it can hardly be construed as unclean or of the devil. It is like refusing to have anything to do with family welfare programmes because some families misuse the funds made available to them.

Furthermore, in 1 Corinthians 5 Paul spells out quite specifically from whom we are to separate. It is not from the ungodly or unrighteous people of the world. The logical outcome of such an attitude would be total withdrawal from the world altogether. That for the apostle is assuredly not a valid option for the Christian. There is no place in the Christian view of life for the voluntary drop-out from society. The separation is rather to be from those who claim to be Christians but whose living reflects the unrighteousness of the person of the world: 'With such a man do not even eat' (1 Cor 5:11).

There are additional arguments to compel the Christian to exercise the right to vote. Appeal may again be made to Jesus' argument based on the use of the coin of the realm. If the Christian is prepared to utilise for business or leisure the currency supported by the government, then he is involved in the life of that government and should be ready to accept the responsibility of such involvement.

Finally, in this matter, the requirement of Romans 13 confronts us. The basic reaction demanded by God's word is submission to the government emerging from acknowledgement that the state is divinely ordained. In a democracy there is a moral obligation to vote, even if it is not laid down as a legal requirement. To cast one's vote is thus a simple act of acknowledging the responsible part God expects us to play in the government of the country where his providence has placed us.

Turning to the wider issue of involvement in the actual political process, we face a much more complex issue, and one where Christians have come to very different conclusions. In practical terms, the matter can be formulated as questions to the individual: Is it right for a Christian to become a member of a political party? Is it right to stand for election, whether at the local government or at the national level? In attempting to answer those questions, I want to view the issue from three standpoints— from that of the church, from that of the ordained minister of the word and from that of the individual church member.

The debate on the church's role in politics revolves around the relationship between the church as the people of God and one particular political party. This has often been a deeply divisive issue and continues to be so. In the nineteenth century, the Church of England was cynically viewed as the Tory party at prayer, while at the same time non-conformity too often appeared as the religious face of the Liberals. In South Africa and Northern Ireland today, there are churches which are openly and unashamedly committed to one particular political stance.

We begin by recalling the fundamental differences between church and state. The role of the church is clearly linked to the work of the gospel. So it may be spelled out in terms of evangelism, edifying the believers and engaging in works of mercy. That is why the characteristic marks of the church have been seen in the area of preaching, worship and congregational discipline. The state by contrast has totally different tasks. It has been set to restrain evil and to promote conditions for stable living. The divergence becomes more marked when we look at the means employed to achieve their ends—for the church the weapons are spiritual and the sanctions are moral, with rebukes to the wrongdoer and ultimately excommunication. For the state, however, government means legal demands and if need be the employment of physical force to achieve ends. The distinction between the two functions is that love is to be the guiding principle in the church, whereas in the state it is law.

The message of the church also diverges from that of the politician. The former is the revelation of the all-knowing and all-wise God and emerges from the infallible word. The political theory, by contrast, is the attempt by fallible men and women to respond to all the complex issues of social and economic life and to discover how relationships, whether within the nation or at an international level, are to be managed. Thus the church aims to tell men and women how to turn to God, how to live as Christians, and how to prepare for heaven. The state has no eternal perspective, but deals with the issues of this life—with farming and fisheries, with education and industry.

For the church to become identified with one political party would be to blur the distinction between the unchanging gospel and the inevitably changing theories of men. Furthermore, if the church is wedded to one political theory, whether capitalist or socialist, it virtually adds another requirement to the gospel. The message to be preached is the call to repentance and faith. If to this is added an unspoken summons to a particular political loyalty, then the church is guilty of adding to the gospel. The letter to the Galatians is not only a vehement denunciation of those in the first century who added a ceremonial requirement to the simple demands of the gospel, it is also a denunciation of those who would add a political requirement. Lest anyone should imagine that this is all a theoretical issue, I refer again to Northern Ireland where there are churches who assume and preach that conversion involves a commitment to a brand of unionist politics, and who would view an evangelical Irish republican as an intolerable hybrid!

Turning to the second area of the debate, there is the role of the preacher. Is it valid for him to be at one and the same time a cleric and a politician? The answer of the bishops of the Middle Ages was 'yes', and there is an equally firm affirmation from those who try to combine the roles of preacher in the pulpit and politician on the hustings. Certainly the apostle Paul would not have recognised this dual role as a valid one. Among his instructions to Timothy, who had been set aside for the work of the gospel, Paul writes firmly: 'No-one serving as a soldier gets involved in civilian affairs—he wants to please his commanding officer. Similarly, if anyone competes as an athlete, he does not receive the victor's crown unless he competes according to the rules' (2 Tim 2:4–5).

I have heard the rather lame justification for the political cleric that Paul was ready to engage in tent-making as well as evangelism. Surely, however, the obvious reason for his occasional recourse to that was simply his need to finance himself when support for his pioneer, and at times lonely, work was not sufficient. He did not travel the country lecturing on tent-making! In fact he was even more explicit: 'I resolved to know nothing while I was with you except Jesus Christ and him crucified' (1 Cor 2:2). One might ask what part of this message involves economic policies for shipbuilding or arming the police for special duties!

There is a further danger in the political preacher. It is that the authority he is given by God as a preacher anointed by the Holy Spirit is too easily transferred in his hearers' minds to his political utterances. When a preacher declares the gospel he speaks with authority because both the message and the authorisation are from heaven. If, however, he chooses to pontificate in some other area, he has no more authority than anyone else, but hearers are in great danger of thinking that wisdom in the gospel means wisdom in other areas. It means nothing of the sort as you would discover to your cost if you entrusted some areas of house repairs to my incompetence!

One final reason for rejecting the alliance of preacher and politician is that his calling is to serve men and women from every background, culture and political persuasion. To confuse the gospel with a political theory could well alienate those who find the politics repellent, and who tragically may reject the gospel because it is presented in the same bundle. Ireland again is an illustration of this where a Bible wrapped in a Union Jack or an Ulster flag will antagonisc a Republican and blind him to a gospel which transcends both unionism and republicanism, and indeed stands in judgement on both!

This does not mean that in a democracy the church has nothing to say on political issues. After all a congregation may number in its membership quite a substantial body of citizens. The total membership of a number of churches in a city will represent a proportion, even though it may be a small one, of the total population. As citizens they are entitled (and in a democratic system are expected) to make their views known.

This, however, is not to be construed as the church pressurising the city council or the member of parliament to gain advantage for its ministry. It must not look to the secular government to support the work of the gospel. Rather it is when there is a moral issue which affects the whole community; then the congregation, like any body of citizens, is entitled to be heard. If there is a club encouraging under-age drinking, or a sex shop peddling pornographic literature, the church can join its voice to the protest of other citizens to demand action. This is not the church trying to gain power of position, but it is rather one more aspect of service to the community as a whole.

The individual Christian may conclude from all this that any political involvement is ruled out. If the church cannot be identified with a particular political theory or party, then surely neither can the church member. This however does not follow! The church as a body has clearly defined tasks and ministries which rule out all kinds of functions which are perfectly legitimate for the believer. Thus the Christian may engage in trade, may be an estate agent or a bank official. Yet clearly it is completely outside the functioning of the church to be involved in the property market or in the buying and selling of goods. The church as a body operates within the sphere of redemption, while the Christian goes out into the world to engage in trade, in business, in leisure activities— and also, if God moves him, into more direct political involvement.

Participating in politics begins for all of us at the level of casting our vote, and at once we face the question: For whom should we vote? Recalling again the earlier reference to 1 Corinthians 5, we need to remember that we should not expect from the man of the world the kind of standard we would expect either from a church member or from an elder within the congregation. We may consult a doctor or a dentist, or do business with a person whose character leaves a lot to be desired. So we may vote for a candidate whose private life may be seriously lacking from a spiritual point of view.

We will ask about the policy of the party he represents. In examining it we will reflect the fact that we hav come to know God personally as the One who has adopted us into his family. We will know from his word that as Creator he has a concern for all men, saint and sinner alike, and sends sunshine and rain to produce the harvest for all and sundry. We will ask therefore whether the political proposals indicate a concern for the community or nation as a whole. A party with a sectional interest will not measure up to this.

Furthermore we will expect an emphasis on social justice. A policy which enriches some and ignores the needs of many, or which sets one part of the country against another, is not a party we will want to support. In this regard we will also recall that our God is the Lord of all the nations. We will therefore be interested not only to know the foreign policy of the party soliciting our vote, but its concern to utilise the resources of an affluent nation to come to the aid of those overseas who, because of natural disasters or commercial entrapment, are irretrievably poor unless some help is given to stimulate their economy.

If the candidate is a Christian we will be profoundly thankful, and may well be ready to vote for him even though he is representing a party which is not our own preference. This is not because we think Christians have a special expertise to enable them to act with superior knowledge. Rather it is that we recognise that one who knows God and knows his word will be governed by the principles of that word, leading to concern for the poor and needy, striving for peace and aiming at social justice. If, however, the Christian is either living a life which belies his profession, or if he is making the disastrous mistake of equating the gospel with his party's programme, then we may well decline to support him.

The further level of involvement, is when the Christian joins a party or becomes a candidate and perhaps ultimately a member of parliament or a government minister. Obviously it is a very difficult path for the Christian. Politicians are often 'economical with the truth', to quote the famous or infamous phrase coined at the *Spycatcher* book trial in Australia. There is that other euphemistic word 'disinformation' which is simply a blurred word to take the place of the blunter 'lies'.

If, however, we go back to the Bible, we find God's people in such situations. In the Old Testament there were men and women of God not only in influential positions in Israel, but also in foreign and pagan courts. One can think of Joseph in Egypt, Daniel in Babylon, Esther and Nehemiah in Persia. Within Israel, in times of godless decline, there were men like Obadiah in Ahab's court whose godliness was lived out in very adverse circumstances. So too in the New Testament there was the centurion whom Jesus so greatly commended, the Ethiopian eunuch serving Queen Candace, and among those mentioned by Paul at the close of his letter written from Rome to the Philippian church—'those who belong to Caesar's household' (Phil 4:22). In none of these cases was there the slightest hint that any of them had compromised their faith by service in a godless regime.

The Christian who embarks at the call of God on this most difficult path—and it will only be at the call of God that he will dare to do so—will be governed by biblical principles. He will echo the concern of the Old and the New Testaments for the poor and the weak, and will be a vigorous spokesman for their needs.

The Christian politician must never forget that he is primarily a Christian. This means that while he recognises the physical and material needs of men and women, he will always see their spiritual needs as being of paramount importance. This should affect his attitude to his political opponents. He may view their policies as inadequate or even positively harmful. He must remember, however, that they themselves desperately need the gospel, and so conduct his opposition to them and their policies that he is still in a position to talk to them person to person about their spiritual needs—just as a Christian shopkeeper will be in competition with business rivals, but must so maintain honesty, integrity and fairness, coupled with Christian courtesy, that he will not close the door to witness to his competitor.

When Paul lists the qualities expected in an elder he insists that 'he must also have a good reputation with outsiders' (1 Tim 3:7). Again he writes of the Christian worker: 'The Lord's servant must not quarrel; instead, he must be kind to everyone' (2 Tim 2:24). Peter has the same emphasis: 'All of you, live in harmony with one another . . . do not repay evil with evil or insult with insult, but with blessing' (1 Pet 3:8–9). Even when facing hostile opponents, the Christian must make a reasoned defence 'with gentleness and respect' (1 Pet 3:16).

These are the very qualities which are appropriate to any Christian in relationships with people at large. They are thus applicable to the Christian politician who engages in the cut and thrust of political debate and operates in an arena where inuendo, misrepresentation and insult are common. The Christian does not need a high rating on the decibel scale to make the point in an argument, nor is he to descend to sarcasm or venom to rebut an opponent's claims. His courtesy in political debate will be an important factor in keeping the door of communication open to share what transcends every political theory, the saving word of Christ.

The Christian in politics must also recognise that someone may be a true believer with a like submission to Scripture and yet be persuaded that another political theory is the better answer to the nation's needs. After all, any political theory is the product of human wisdom and is liable to be adjusted to changing circumstances. In this respect it is utterly unlike the unchanging gospel. The Christian must not assume that his political theorising perfectly reflects the mind of the Creator. A measure of humility here will not only check the temptation to unjustified dogmatism, but will also give him a greater readiness to recognise that a brother or sister may differ radically from his views and yet remain a beloved fellow Christian.

8

Pornography, Perversion and Censorship

There has never been a time when whole nations were so bombarded with all kinds of pornography, whether so-called soft or hard. No previous generation had such a variety of media, since magazines and newspapers have now been joined by radio, television and cassettes—both sound and video. The advent of satellite TV promises an even greater assault on the moral fibre of people who will be able to flood their living rooms with every kind of filth which the perverted minds of men can produce.

It is perhaps not surprising that the flood of obscenity threatens to overflow when we realise how much money there is in the business. Behind the tabloid newspapers, salacious magazines and perverted videos, there are callous operators whose god is money, whose moral standards are seemingly non-existent and whose astute business sense tells them that there is a vast market awaiting their productions. I recall visiting someone years back in a very up-market suburban estate in South London. The man turned out to be the night editor of one of the leading national tabloid papers. His wife, perhaps rather conscious of being landed with a minister, or maybe simply trying to preserve her middle-class image, was somewhat embarrassed. Her husband was far from feeling like that. Indeed his cynical comment was that he gave people what they wanted.

It is not surprising that periodically there are calls for censorship, and indeed attempts have been made. The press council adjudicates, but one fears its teeth are like false dentures which can be removed when the situation requires. Governments try to find a balance between the freedom of the press and the corrupting of the nation, between controlling the kind of films which they judge intolerable and leaving things to run their course. Politics are seen clearly in this area to be the art of the possible. Great numbers are glad to spend their Sunday mornings sampling the moral sludge dredged up for them by cynical journalists. These people have votes and there is always the reality of a general election. So it is with faltering steps that governments act.

In fairness one must add that it is not such a simple matter. Who is to be the judge as to what is obscene? The very word has been analysed in the courts where this difficulty of definition has often been exploited by defence lawyers. It refers to any material written or visual which tends to deprave or corrupt. That however applies not only to portrayals of sexual perversion but to the glorification of violence and brutal unconcern for others. Racially-biased productions attempt to elicit hate for other ethnic groups—are these not as obscene as pornographic films?

How is the Christian to react? Has the church a public role in the battle against obscenity? We are back with the basic issue of the Christian's role in society. While in Paul's words our citizenship is in heaven, and while Peter describes us as foreigners, yet our relationship to our country is not simply like a foreigner in some nation not his own. The Briton living in another country must clearly abide by the laws of that country, but he has no right or responsibility to try and get the laws of that land changed. The Christian, however, while having his primary loyalty to his heavenly King, must also function as a citizen here. This means not only obeying the laws of the land, but acting as a responsible citizen by objecting to breaches of the law, and where the law is not clear or explicit, trying by every legitimate means to persuade the law-makers to legislate firmly against corruption.

It will not do to say that you cannot make bad people good by law. That is perfectly true. You can, however, restrain bad people from corrupting others. The Christian police officer knows perfectly well that the criminal needs the gospel and a transforming work of God. Yet he also has a responsibility to track down and arrest that same criminal to protect society. The prison officer who is a Christian knows that the inmates need the liberty which Christ brings, but he also knows that society needs a continuing protection. So the Christian citizen is fully aware that only the grace of God will change the perverted appetites of fallen men, but meanwhile society has to be protected from the worst excesses of the purveyors of filth.

Living in two worlds at the same time is one of the great problems of being a Christian. It means in this matter of active involvement in society that we have to recognise that we simply cannot impose the same restraints on men and women in general that we expect to see imposed within the church. Christians are confronted with the ultimate standard of Jesus: 'Be perfect, therefore, as your heavenly Father is perfect' (Mt 5:48). This means that the thought life of the believer is under the scrutiny of heaven: 'Put to death, therefore, whatever belongs to your earthly nature: sexual immorality, impurity, lust, evil desires and greed, which is idolatry' (Col 3:5). So too conversation and the whole pattern of conduct must be censored: 'You must rid yourselves of . . . slander and filthy language from your lips' (Col 3:8). 'Nor should there be obscenity, foolish talk or coarse joking, which are out of place, but rather thanksgiving' (Eph 5:4). 'Have nothing to do with the fruitless deeds of darkness, but rather expose them. For it is shameful even to mention what the disobedient do in secret' (Eph 5:11–12).

By God's grace the Christian may aim at these standards, not only personally but also for those for whom he or she may have some measure of responsibility. Thus a Christian parent within the framework of family life may refuse to tolerate certain newspapers or magazines and may insist on a control of TV or video programmes to be seen within the home. In the wider context of church life, there will be the godly discipline which not only requires members to aim at the highest standards, but is ready to act firmly if any member is falling seriously short, and even more firmly if the failure is corrupting others.

However, in the context of society at large there is not the recognition of the absolute requirements of God. 'The sinful mind is hostile to God. It does not submit to God's law, nor can it do so' (Rom 8:7). There are limits therefore to the moral demands which can be made and to the restraints on personal freedom which will be tolerated. The reaction of some may be to shrug the shoulders and feel relieved of responsibility. The Christian cannot do this. Called to be a good citizen he sees his responsibility to men and women at large.

After all, if there was an open sewer with grim potential for the spread of disease he would have little hesitation in adding his signature to a district petition demanding that the local council take action. Likewise, if the moral cesspool is uncovered, his concern for the moral health of society will make him ready to act. He is fully aware that good health will not save men and women, and good moral standards will not transform their hearts. Yet he is a servant of the God who 'causes his sun to rise on the evil and the good, and sends rain on the righteous and the unrighteous' (Mt. 5:45). Hence the Christian, with full awareness that he is only dealing with the symptoms of a disease, will yet engage in that necessary amelioration of human wretchedness.

As in other areas of social concern, the Christian will be prepared to act in conjunction with non-Christians. Reverting to the illustration of the open sewer, he knows pagan or atheist neighbours who have a deep concern for the health of their children and indeed for the community at large. So he has no difficulty in joining forces with them. Why then should he be hesitant about a campaign to clean up moral filth which is even more injurious to the health of the community?

While the Christian may join forces with citizens at large, he has an advantage in that he knows the God who has created all of them. Furthermore, he knows from God's book what the true nature of man is. He reads in that same book of God's concern for the integrity of marriage, for the well-being of family life, for the protection of the weak and the poor. Thus he has a clearer perspective on the needs of the community and recognises the seeds of corruption in their earliest manifestation. The Christian agriculturist, for example, knows that the only ultimate answer to human needs is the bread of life, but meantime he is also concerned to feed the hungry with good crops. The knowledge of the Creator gives him a distinctive insight into the whole process of growth and an awareness of the activity of the God who gives the harvest. Yet he still works with non-Christian colleagues who, with a total blindness to the glory of God in the world around, may yet show great concern to help Third World peoples share in the green revolution.

In many such areas of social concern Christians are active. It will however soon become clear that social concern inevitably impinges on political issues since the only way of restraining wrong-doing and compelling reasonable social behaviour is legislation. So the Christian will support any movement to censor what is obscene and therefore injurious to society at large, especially those like children and young people who are particularly vulnerable.

One objection to any form of censorship is the appeal to literary or artistic merit. When the famous trial took place over the novel of D H Lawrence *Lady Chatterley's Lover* this was a major argument in the legal defence. This however must be exposed for what it is, namely another version of a well-worn argument that the end justifies the means. On this basis one could justify nearly any production. If gross sexual perversion was presented by superb acting and outstanding photography, would that make it acceptable? It is as facile and empty an argument as the claim of the Nazi doctors in the concentration camps who used human victims as guinea pigs to further investigation into disease. We would react with utter revulsion and insist that medical advance by such means is totally unacceptable. Equally unacceptable is the corrupting of those who act and those who watch in the alleged quest for artistic excellence.

A further objection comes from those who protest at any infringement of personal liberty. This is again a specious protest since society can only continue to function by restraining freedom where the exercise of that freedom is harmful to others. The whole range of traffic laws illustrate the need for curtailing personal liberty. A motorist may wish to drive a powerful car at high speed through a built-up area. A drunken driver may insist with blurred speech on his freedom to do as he chooses with his own car. We readily see that curtailing freedom in such matters is a social necessity. What we need to do is to persuade the legislators that there is a like need for legal restraints in other areas of equal concern.

Censorship does not only involve issues of sex. Christians indeed are rightly criticised when their only concern seems to be with sexual matters, whereas violence and racial hatred are also deeply obscene. However, having recognised that danger, one must also insist on the especially grave nature of sexual perversion in that it attacks the very fabric of society. It does this by undermining the concept of faithfulness within marriage and so attacking the most basic social unit, namely the family.

There is another feature in sexual wrong-doing which marks it out as distinct. Paul points out that: 'All other sins a man commits are outside his body, but he who sins sexually sins against his own body' (1 Cor 6:18). For the Christian, that is an especially serious matter in view of Paul's words which follow: 'Do you not know that your body is a temple of the Holy Spirit, who is in you, whom you have received from God?' (v 19). To sin sexually is thus to defile God's temple and so to sin against the resident in that temple, namely the Holy Spirit.

Clearly the person who does not have the Spirit of God is not in that position. Yet because the body is the gift of the Creator, and because man made in the image of God requires the body to reflect the glory of that message, there is a sanctity attached to the human body. Because the Creator designed that body in such a way that a man and a woman could come together in physical union, the very act of sexual intercourse is a fulfilment of the divine purpose in creation. There is therefore a particular seriousness in violating that purpose.

God's answer to sin is wrath, which means not some arbitrary loss of temper, but an inflexible refusal to countenance unrighteousness and an imposition of penalties on those who disobey. These penalties include the physical consequences of sexual immorality. The long medical history of venereal diseases, culminating in the twentieth-century scourge AIDS, takes us back to Paul's sombre reflection that those who refuse God's pattern 'received in themselves the due penalty for their perversion' (Rom 1:27).

As an informed citizen, the Christian has a duty to point out that sexual immorality has implications for society. There is the family tragedy where one partner in a marriage is infected by the disease incurred by the other partner's wrong-doing. There is the tragedy of children born with serious defects inherited from parental misuse of the gift of sex. There is the enormous extra burden placed on medical and hospital resources by illness acquired through wilful sexual sin, and this means a diminution in medical provision for other forms of serious sickness.

Literature or visual arts which present and glory in sexual aberrations and perversions carry a heavy responsibility. If the titillating pictures and stories are constantly presented to people's minds and senses, it is no wonder that passions are aroused. If sex is a fun game for personal pleasure, it is no surprise to discover that gratification is seen as the goal to be sought. The disastrous outcome is seen in many shattered lives.

There are other serious social consequences which it is the Christian's responsibility to highlight. As the barriers of what is permitted are broken down so the lusts of men and women will want more. Where they are not able to have their pleasure by the willing consent of others they will take what they want by force if need be. It is no surprise therefore that the so-called sexual revolution has occurred at the same time as the perverted misuse of children for sexual purposes. The word 'paedophile' is a grotesque misnomer for one who sexually abuses children. The word literally means 'child lover', yet no one could possibly be so described who would violate the most intimate area of a child's body or an adolescent's life.

It is also a fact that much of this kind of literature presents women as sexual objects for men to gratify their instincts. The biblical view of sexual union as the loving climax of self-giving by two people is replaced by that of someone utilising another person's body. Whether it is the payment of a prostitute who is often forced by economic pressure into the trade, or whether it is the violence of rape, in both cases it is a grievous violation not only of an individual but of the very framework of society.

Someone may object that the Christian has little justification for wanting to limit the literary or visual depiction of sexual activity, in view of the Bible's explicit descriptions of and at times glorying in the female body. The story of Onan is quite explicit in its description of physical details. The Song of Songs has been interpreted by generations of Christians as a series of poems declaring the love of Christ for his people. Nonetheless it is very expressive of the beauty of the bride's body and indeed exhibits a clearly declared delight in enjoying the physical beauty of that body. The objector may ask what the difference is between these and other passages, and what is termed soft pornography.

By way of reply one must note the difference between prudery and modesty. Prudery is an attitude which will hardly mention basic bodily functions, much less the experience of sexual delight. Modesty, which is what one encounters in the Bible, is not ashamed of the physical beauty of the human body whether male or female. Christian modesty likewise does not refer to sex in an oblique and shamefaced way, but rather rejoices that it was the Creator himself who linked sex with pleasure.

The Bible however is as far removed as possible from pornography, soft or hard, in that it limits sexual pleasure to the intimacy of marriage. It does not countenance casual sex, but insists on chastity. It insists also on restraint—even within marriage. Above all it rejects the notion of seeing another's body as being solely for our pleasure. In fact at the heart of biblical teaching on sex is the concept of self-giving and self-sacrifice. It is as a husband or wife seeks primarily the fulfilment and happiness of the other that they discover their own.

One cannot deal with this area of sexual sin without being confronted with the issue of homosexuality. Attitudes generally have greatly altered with the legalising of homosexual acts in private between consenting adults. For many it is all a matter of inherited personal sexual orientation. As a result it is a question of individual choice and any criticism of the practice is viewed as being intolerant and indeed akin to such evils as racial prejudice.

In facing this issue the Christian must remember the difference between a sin and a crime, and also the distinction between condemnation of sin and continuing concern for the sinner. Take the first difference—between sin and crime. Many actions are sinful, but they only become criminal when the state declares them to be such. Thus adultery is a grievous sin in God's sight, but it is not a criminal offence. Covetousness is a sin, but only when it leads to theft does the action become criminal. The Christian will see a much more widespread presence of sin and indeed recognises it in his own life. He will however only be ready to join with others in calling for legislation when the particular sin is such as to harm others—society, the family and ultimately the nation. As he moves along this line he will aim to reflect the love of Christ who could exhibit such love and tenderness while yet being very clear and emphatic in his judgement on sin and his call to the sinner to repent.

There are further factors to keep in mind. While in Romans 1 homosexuality is presented as a grievous sin, it is by no means the only sin and so must never have so much concentrated attention and condemnation that other ugly manifestations of fallen human nature are forgotten. Furthermore, the gospel is an essential remedy for all sinners, whatever the particular symptoms of their sinfulness. The doctor treating the patient suffering from VD may be faithful in his own marriage, but he needs the gospel as much as the patient. The nurse may have resisted the current drift and remained a virgin, but she needs a Saviour as truly as the promiscuous patient.

In the Bible, homosexual activity is again and again declared to be an abomination in the sight of God. This is against the background of the very positive view of sex as the gift of God. When Jesus dealt with the marriage/divorce issue he went back to the creation narrative where the design was that a man and a woman should become 'one flesh'. For Paul there was something so beautiful and sacred in the sexual relationship of a man and a woman that he could use it as a picture of the most holy relationship of Christ and his church.

By contrast with this positive extolling of sex, the Bible

consistently rejects homosexuality. Sodom, the city which gave its name to the practice, is seen as an example of particularly flagrant sinfulness. 'Now the men of Sodom were wicked and were sinning greatly against the Lord' (Gen 13:13). 'The outcry against Sodom and Gomorrah is so great and their sin so grievous' (Gen 18:20). Jude in his epistle describes the sins of Sodom as 'sexual immorality and perversion' (v 7). Leviticus is equally explicit: 'Do not lie with a man as one lies with a woman; that is detestable ... Everyone who does any of these detestable things—such persons must be cut off from their people ... If a man lies with a man as one lies with a woman, both of them have done what is detestable' (Lev 18:22,29; 20:13).

Paul deals specifically with the practice on various occasions. He sees it as a practice in which men dishonour their bodies in that they use them in a way which their Creator clearly never intended them to be used. Just as the book of Judges recorded the sordid story of the unbridled homosexuality of Gibeah as a sign of the moral decadence of the nation, so Paul speaks of the practice as being the final stage in moral deviation (Judg 19:22–25; Rom 1:26–32). When he recalled the Corinthians' past it is in the context of a stern reminder that among other categories of offenders neither 'male prostitutes nor homosexual offenders' will inherit the kingdom of God. Then he adds: 'And that is what some of you were. But you were washed, you were sanctified, you were justified in the name of the Lord Jesus Christ and by the Spirit of our God' (1 Cor 6:11).

All this however is dealing with the realm of sin, but in the political arena we have to address a wider issue. Is it right to attempt to frame laws, or to persuade legislators to do so, to restrain the propagation of the practice? In practical terms is it valid not only to call the homosexual to repent and turn to Christ, but also to call for censorship of literature glorifying the practice, or video cassettes or TV programmes with a similar goal? Should Christians in short have applauded or deplored Clause 28 which was added as an amendment to a government bill forbidding local councils to encourage the deliberate advocacy

of homosexuality? It is my deep conviction that such an amendment should have firm support.

We reject the claim that this is some kind of witch hunt since
we are not dealing with private personal practice but with a very
public and increasingly aggressive homosexual and lesbian lobby
which demands more and more rights. Hence the campaign of
the so-called gay liberation front aims to make homosexual
practice equally acceptable with what not only the Bible but the
great majority of people see as normal sexual relationships.
Hence there are also attacks on churches or Christian agencies
who will not employ practising homosexuals. There is also an
attempt to deprive of charitable status any agencies which will
not capitulate to the endorsement of homosexual practice.

This is not a Christian lobby trying to fasten New Testament
standards on a pagan nation. Indeed it is most significant that
when a Baptist minister took a public stand in Harringay over
this issue he had huge support from non-Christians. In fact it is
again an example of the Christian citizen, aware of the Creator's
design for men and women, attempting to alert the community to
those elements which make for family breakdown and thus social
disintegration.

The social injuries inflicted on others call not only for attention,
but also action. It is clear that the main reservoir of AIDS
infection is the homosexual community. The government which
tries to make this a practical rather than a moral issue refers to
'high-risk groups'. Such groups however include many who are
bisexual with wives put at risk. They also include those who gave
blood for transfusions, hence the desperate tragedy of haemophiliacs receiving infected blood. It is not so-called safe sex which
is required, but chastity with a marriage relationship of one man
and one woman. Is there to be no moral indignation at the plight
of wives doomed to die of AIDS because of their husbands'
perversion, or of haemophiliacs facing death because they were
fatally infected from a source totally outside their control? In all
the clamour for homosexual rights there is a dearth of compassion
for the innocent victims.

Environmental health has become a major issue in our day.

Agitation is intense and lobbying is keen—and justifiably so—to check the unrestricted misuse of the land, the sea and the atmosphere. There are very vociferous groups with whom one must deeply sympathise who wish to see controls imposed on the emission of noxious fumes from factories and power stations; on dangerous effluent from chemical plants, on wanton dumping of poisonous materials. It is equally important to insist on mental health and moral well-being, and to resist the selfish interest groups who want either financial profit or twisted pleasure, however deeply others may be harassed. Censorship is simply legal control of the foul emissions of corrupting material which not only depraves the minds of readers or viewers, but finally rots the very fibre of society. The Christian who is a responsible citizen should be ready to use his pen or his voice to join with other responsible citizens to check a deluge of filth which threatens to engulf us all.

9

Crime, Punishment and the Death Penalty

In an ideal world there would be no need for punishment, but then there would be no crime. We, however, do not live in an ideal world, but in the real world where sin has reigned since the dawn of history, or more precisely since the lure of personal pleasure and advantage drew Adam and Eve away from obedience to God. Thus obedience was already the pattern of a truly ideal world, but its tragic change to disobedience introduced the principle of selfishness and personal ambition which has led and still leads countless men and women into serious wrong-doing.

Such wrong-doing is anti-social. It deprives others of their goods, their property or even their lives. When it is fraud perpetrated against a government, it can easily be seen, though mistakenly so, as simply getting the better of a rather remote institution. In fact it is just as anti-social since it robs the government of the tax or revenue which might otherwise be used to benefit the people, either directly through the welfare arrangements for the needy, or indirectly through the provision of necessary social amenities, such as transport facilities, fresh water, sewage disposal and so on. The criminal, whether he be a burglar with a jemmy or a city financier with a computer, is therefore basically a selfish, anti-social individual who needs to be deterred from his wrong-doing.

The first major issue of debate to arise is the nature of punishment. At this stage we are not discussing modes of punishment such as custodial sentences over against compulsory social service. Nor have we yet come to the issue of capital punishment.

Before these can be discussed with any degree of understanding we must face the more basic issue as to what is implied in the very concept of punishment.

There is a very strong and influential body of opinion today which insists that punishment must only be seen as remedial. The primary aim in dealing with the wrong-doer is his or her re-formation. There is an admission that of course there is a need to protect society from the vicious or unscrupulous, though at times one has an uneasy feeling that so much attention is paid to the criminal that the plight of the victims and their dread of further injury tends to have a secondary place. Yet even when there is concern for the victim there is still the vigorous contention that what is required from the criminal is not that retribution be exacted, but that he should be restored to society as a different man with different aims and with his anti-social attitudes firmly rejected.

The argument tends to be buttressed by the use of pejorative or loaded language. Read the correspondence or articles on the subject in one of the so-called quality newspapers, and you find the writers accusing those who disagree with them of indulging a primitive desire for revenge. There is a grotesque caricature of vindictive and angry lobbyists out to exact an eye for an eye and a tooth for a tooth. They claim that the call for punishment of offenders is like the blood letting of a vendetta such as has been seen in the wilder areas of Sardinia. When the debate turns to the question of the death penalty there is even greater outrage whose favourite term of abuse seems to be that it is an obscenity.

Many of us will have a distinctly dubious attitude to the kind of argument which has to be buttressed by this kind of language. It savours of the preachers whose thin arguments are reinforced by increased volume as if shouting was the ultimate support of logic and homiletical hollering was the guarantee of sound theology. What is needed is first of all to examine the roots of the approach which dismisses retribution and then to turn to the biblical analysis.

Those who maintain this position would claim that it is a humane standpoint, and at first they may seem to be justified in their claim. It is, they would insist, a mark of a civilised people that they move away from the primitive savagery of their ancestors to a much more rational way of dealing with problems. Again they have a point. Indeed, those who argue for retribution as an essential element in punishment must always be on the alert to ensure that their convictions are rooted in biblical argument and reasoned discussion rather than in the blindly irrational urge which easily arises in face of some brutal crime.

This morning, before I wrote this chapter, I listened to the early morning radio news. One grim item told of what is all too common: the murder of an old lady in her own home, doubtless for the purpose of stealing money for drugs or drink. What added horror to the story was that she had dialled 999 when she heard the intruder and the police officer heard her screams as she was attacked. Any normal human being is utterly revolted by such callous brutality and certainly there can be an emotional reaction. Yet such revulsion must not be dismissed so lightly as being an irrational urge for vengeance.

It is surely part of our humanity that we feel deeply and even passionately in face of the exploitation, injury and degrading of the weak and the aged. Such emotional reaction is justified, yet nonetheless it still needs to be kept within the bounds of clear thinking. Feelings out of control can be as bad or worse than indifference. Such feelings lead to lynch law and down that path lies the peril of innocent victims of blind fury and ultimately chaos. We are not called on to be cold, calculating machines, nor are we to be uncontrolled in our emotional outbursts. We are to think clearly and yet we will inevitably feel deeply, and both of these reactions are needed.

Behind the current call for humane methods of punishment, with its rejection of anything savouring of retribution, is the humanist view of men and women. Humanism, as its name suggests, begins and ends in its thinking with the human situation. That means that there is no reference to any being outside the human condition, whether God or devil. Hence any appeal to a divinely-revealed law is rejected. Indeed, any suggestion of moral absolutes is inevitably ruled out. The ultimate concern is human well-being and the only means to ascertain how this may be achieved and preserved is human reflection prompting human attitudes and human action. God's word simply is not on the agenda.

As well as these basic humanist presuppositions, there are also the ideas derived from the theory of biological evolution. The scientific theory is that man has evolved over vast tracts of time from very primitive origins. However, there has developed a whole philosophy which sees also a cultural and moral development. Thus primitive man living by brute force in the context of nature, red in tooth and claw has given way, albeit very slowly, to developed civilised man. Sadly, the proponents of this view have to admit that traces of our savage ancestry still persist and have to be dealt with if we are all going to survive. Those who transgress are not to be seen as evil or wicked, but as those who need to be taught their responsibility to live aright within society.

There are deep-seated fallacies in the whole argument. In the first place, there is an underlying error which reaches right back to the philosophy of ancient Greece, namely that knowledge means ability. This, however, is only true to a limited extent. It is certainly true that someone who has mastered the intricacies of a car engine is able to do repairs which otherwise would have to be left to the mechanics. It is true that knowledge of a foreign language means ability to communicate with people of another country. But when we come to the area of conduct, and to decisions of what is right and wrong, the idea breaks down. The dishonest financier knows perfectly well how to operate in the market and what are the benefits which accrue. Yet he embezzles and defrauds because his covetousness and greed stoke his ambition to reap excessive dividends, and this involves dishonesty.

Behind much of the exclusive emphasis on the remedial element in punishment is what can only be described as a naive view of human nature. It is the notion that if only we can show people what is good and right they will choose what is good and do what is right. The blunt reality is that this simply does not follow. The swindlers, the highly-professional crooks, the twisted lawyers, the bent policemen—all of these know what is right. Some of them indeed are supposed to be part of the process of guarding the rights of society, and yet selfishness turns their knowledge in the wrong direction. Education may lead to more civilised and cultured living, but it also leads to much more clever criminals.

A further fallacy in the humanist diagnosis is that they view the wrong-doer as basically sick. If only he was a healthy-minded individual he would behave reasonably to his fellow human beings and recognise how wrong it is to rob or injure the society of which he is a part. It is thus the function of the courts to discover, with the aid of skilled psychologists, what are the causes of the mental aberration of the criminal. It is the task of the prison or probation services, with the help of expert psycho-therapists, to decide the therapy which is required before the criminal—or perhaps more correctly from this standpoint the patient—is returned to society.

This all seems so reasonable and humane and morally far superior to the alleged barbarism of those who say that retribution is an essential ingredient. On the one side are the proponents of a view which claims that the only possible considerations are the desire to protect society and the hope of restoring the wrong-doer. On the other side, those who argue that the wrong-doer should reap the due consequences of his wrong-doing are maligned as at best trapped in past attitudes and at worst motivated by the blind urge for revenge.

We must ask however if this so-called humane view is really humane at all. The late C S Lewis wrote a brilliant and penetrating essay on the subject, published first in Australia because he found an unreadiness to publish it in Britain and then reprinted in the quarterly journal *The Churchman*. The title was 'The Humanitarian Theory of Punishment' which its proponents con-sidered 'mild and merciful', but which he judged to lead to 'the possibility of cruelty and injustice without end'. One needs to read the essay to appreciate the devastating impact of his argu-ments. I can only pick out some salient points in his trenchant critique of humanist views and his sturdy and unashamed emphasis on the notion of the criminal getting what he deserves.

Lewis contended with great vigour that it is only retribution which recognises human dignity. To punish a man because he deserves it is to appeal to his conscience and to the conscience of the community. It is to treat him as a being made in the image of God. The supposedly humane theory operates with a totally different approach. He is sick and needs first of all to recognise his sickness in order that he may be cured.

Who then is to diagnose his sickness? The old view summoned a jury of ordinary folk who listened to the arguments, were guided by the judge as the expert referee, but who then came to their own reasoned verdict. The humanitarian view places the whole process in the hands of the expert psychologist whose diagnosis depends on some school of thought and whose methods of treatment are influenced by his theories. Yet as Lewis pointed out, the 'cure' is as compulsory as the older imprisonment. The difference is that the sentence handed down by a judge is at least theoretically conforming to notions of justice and injustice so that two centuries ago when unreasonable sentences were being imposed, juries of honest-thinking citizens refused to convict and the law had to be changed. The expert psychotherapist does not have such sanctions. He and his fellows move in a realm whose expertise is not the common property of ordinary mortals. They therefore must decide when treatment is complete. The patient is at their mercy.

Furthermore, as Lewis so trenchantly pointed out, the whole idea of deterring others becomes totally immoral. If I am 'sick' in the view of the experts and my 'treatment' is being forced on me, I am entitled to protest. By what criterion of justice am I to be used as a means to an end to deter others? If in fact I am in the old view a wrong-doer and am receiving my just deserts, then I have no grounds for complaint. The deterrent effect to others is the spin off, but the essential reason for my punishment is my own wrong-doing. With all its weakness, the judicial system does attempt to make the punishment fit the crime. So it imposes a penalty on which the criminal can reflect and to which outsiders may give heed. But both the remedial effects on him and the deterrent effect on them are secondary to the main purpose of punishment, namely to declare publicly that wrong-doing is evil and should be dealt with firmly but also fairly.

'The humanitarian theory, then,' wrote Lewis, 'removes sentences from the hands of jurists whom the public is entitled to criticise and places them in the hands of technical experts whose special sciences do not even employ such categories as rights or justice.' That, however, is not the only serious flaw, for there is worse to follow! The fact that those responsible for the wrongdoer's or perhaps I should say the patient's rehabilitation may be deeply sincere. Yet history displays in vivid colours how sincerity can be a more terrifying prospect for someone who is at the mercy of that sincerity than ordinary violence from others. The latter, like the bully, may lose interest or turn their attention elsewhere. The sincere exponents of some theory, however, will feel that they have a solemn duty to carry out to the uttermost their task. Doubtless some of the fiendish tortures of the Spanish Inquisition were inflicted by men whose perverted minds sincerely felt they were working for their victims' eternal good, even if their present bodily condition had to be sacrificed. When, as inevitably happens in any society, the sincere give way to the ruthless, the 'humane' view ends with the horrors of Stalin's psychiatric wards so brilliantly reflected in George Orwell's famous novel *Nineteen Eighty-four*.

Since for many psychologists religion is itself a neurosis, one can understand their further conclusion that it is anti-social. As with any contagious disease, those affected need to be removed for treatment. Since religious belief is judged to be a mental illness, the answer must be to try and cure these alleged superstitions by eradicating the false thinking and setting the patient on the path to mental health and normality. Normality, it may be added, is what in this theory the experts or more significantly their political masters judge to be such. This is not humane, but grossly inhuman. The blunt name for the treatment is not mental therapy, but brainwashing. Yet it is important to emphasise that the ugly excesses of these assaults on human personality emerged from the apparently mild and merciful and eminently reasonable theories of those who reacted against the alleged barbarism of retribution.

The Bible is totally clear in this matter. Retribution is of the essence of all punishment. It is so because God says it is! This however is not to brush aside all questions and to substitute a bold appeal to an external edict. God himself does not thus declare it. Rather he appeals to the thinking of the men and women he addresses. His approach is reflected in the call that comes to sinners in the opening prophecy of Isaiah: '"Come now, let us reason together," says the Lord' (Is 1:18).

God appeals to our mind with rational arguments. He did this in the Garden of Eden. Having presented to Adam and Eve the rich potential of the garden for their pleasure and satisfaction, he then made clear the firm requirement laid down for their good and the inevitable consequence of disobedience. When in face of their wilfulness he sentenced them to exclusion from the garden and hard labour within a corrupted creation, the sentence was handed down by rational means. They were to see the link between wrong-doing and painful consequence. The reason why God could thus appeal to them with argument, and why they were able to recognise the logic of their punishment, was that God had created them in his image.

Retribution is thus not a degrading of the criminal. Rather it maintains and enhances his essential human dignity. It works on the principle that he should be brought to recognise the evil of his deeds. Society is represented in the jury by his own peer group of fellow humans. The fact that they come to the conclusion that he is guilty should bring home to him the seriousness of what he has done. He is not therefore being reduced to the level of a psychological problem. He is rather a moral being, responsible for his actions and so justifiably subjected to the consequences in terms of a penalty.

It is only in the framework of retribution that mercy and pardon have any real meaning. If a man is ill you may show sympathy, pity or concern, but you cannot show mercy since in the humanist argument he is not culpable. So too the pardon which can intervene to remit or mitigate punishment is only understandable against the background of a broken law and a guilty wrong-doer. If a man's conduct is simply the by-product of his genes, his upbringing and his environment, you cannot pardon him, for such a pardon would introduce the notions of blame and guilt. You may be kind to him, but kindness enforced by others against our wills, and indeed in defiance of what we ourselves judge to be right, is no kindness at all. It is in fact to dethrone us as responsible human beings and to inflict on us intolerable injustice. C S Lewis well sums it up: 'Mercy detached from justice becomes unmerciful.'

Going back to the biblical view of the state in Romans 13 we find the distinction between 'what is right' and 'what is wrong'. It is the responsibility of the state to punish what is wrong, not simply to deter others, nor to reform the wrong-doer, but essentially because of the evil nature of his deed. In this, the state authority is the 'agent of wrath to bring punishment on the wrong-doer' (Rom 13:4). Behind the law and the system of justice which upholds the law and by punishment vindicates it, there stands a greater tribunal. The background of this passage in chapter 13 is in fact the whole developed argument of this great letter to the church in Rome.

This means that to understand the teaching on the retributive justice administered by the judicial system, we must retrace our steps to hear God's verdict on humanity. The opening chapters of God's word speak of men and women standing under the authority of their Creator. He has written his just law on the hearts of all men, and in specific detail in the Old Testament law. This is why every excuse is stopped and all the world stands guilty before God. Since it was guilt not disease which had to be dealt with, God honoured his law by the willing sacrifice of his Son who recognised both the universal breach of that law and the justifiable retribution by himself taking the guilt and accepting the penalty. Retribution lies at the heart of the gospel and mercy is seen in all its wonder at the cross since it was at Calvary that justice and mercy kissed one another.

It is this serious view of God's law which leads not only to a solemn fear in face of God's wrath, and not only to an admission that the condemnation and the penalty due to sinners is fully justified; it leads also to a glad and grateful amazement at the richness of God's mercy. It is thus against a background of the gospel expression of God's retribution that Paul expounds the role of the state.

The criminal facing sentence is facing a sentence of a human judge, but even though the latter may through human prejudice or corruption mar the judgement yet even in a distorted way it reflects a pattern derived from heaven. Happy is the nation whose judges have their roots in the biblical heritage and who try to the best of their ability to echo the sentence of the heavenly Judge, and in sentencing to reflect the attitude of heaven by tempering justice with mercy.

This brings us to the most controversial issue of all—whether the state has the right to impose the death penalty as the ultimate penalty for the ultimate crime of murder. Those who argue against capital punishment assert that to execute a human being is simply to respond to violence with violence and to reply to murder with judicial killing. Some proponents will react emotionally and will with emotive language speak of the hangman's noose or the guillotine as the supreme obscenity. Others will try to reason with cooler heads and with compelling arguments that it can never be right to take another human life, no matter how terrible the crime of that person has been.

We must not over-react and imply that those who reject capital punishment are somehow condoning murder and showing scant regard or sympathy for the victim or the grief-stricken relatives. We must listen to arguments without attributing wrong motives, though we may justifiably argue that while the proponents of this view may be serious and take crime very seriously indeed, yet the arguments and the conclusion drawn tend to cheapen the value of human life. However, since that can be a two-edged argument in that they may reply that the death penalty also cheapens human life, we would prefer to turn to biblical evidence.

Before examining that evidence it would seem important to clarify some issues and to deal with some of the arguments. At each parliamentary session there is an attempt to restore the death sentence to British administration of justice as it has been restored in some of the states in the USA. The arguments on both sides usually fail to deal with the central issue, in that consideration of retribution is largely ignored not only in parliament but in the discussion and correspondence carried in the news media.

Much of the debate has focused on the question of whether the death sentence is really a deterrent. On the one hand the police and many others would argue that the fear of it would deter many a criminal from carrying a gun and they would cite the appalling rise in crimes involving violence and death. On the other hand it is pointed out that a great many murders are committed in a fit of rage or passion and would not be subject to rational restraint.

The argument as to whether it is a deterrent or not is buttressed by the appeal to statistical evidence. Some point to a rising murder rate where the death penalty is removed, while others cite statistics to show that in countries where this has happened the rate has in fact not risen or has even fallen. Many of us are somewhat dubious about the use of statistics which can so easily be manipulated to try to win an argument. In any case, as I tried to argue earlier in this chapter, one can only really discuss the issue of deterrence after the basic matter of retribution is dealt with.

Another attempt to evade the problem follows the line that while the right of the state to impose the death penalty should be maintained yet in fact it should rarely if ever be carried out. The late Emil Brunner, the continental theologian, followed this line and seemed to be trying to get the best of both worlds. He wrote in his massive book on Christian ethics: 'It is, of course, true that the state does possess the right to kill, and to contest this means to destroy the power of the state ... but this right should be hedged about with so many restrictions that practically it would not exist.'[5] One can only comment that if a practice is right then it should be employed. To try and maintain and deny at the same time is an ethical sleight of hand which simply does not convince.

One other very serious problem must be faced, and that is the possibility of executing an innocent person. Admittedly this may be a quite remote possibility, but no matter how remote it is such a dreadful prospect that it must be taken into consideration. If therefore there is any possibility of a mistaken verdict then assuredly the death sentence is ruled out. A re-trial or a royal pardon is a possibility even after years in prison, but it is completely ruled out if the prisoner is executed.

Turning then to the biblical evidence, we must examine in more detail what Paul had to say in Romans 13 about the punitive element in the administration of justice by the state. He uses the vivid metaphor of bearing the sword. Someone may argue that this is pictorial language and it is invalid to press such a phrase into a hard literalistic mould. So they might point to the day some years ago when there was a famous dismissal of ministers in a very drastic cabinet re-shuffle. It was referred to as 'the night of the long knives'. In the same way, a journalist will describe a fierce trade union argument or a bitter political quarrel and comment that there was blood on the floor. In neither case was any physical damage done!

However, one must examine this objection more closely. Knives, with their consequent blood letting, are not the actual weapons used in our current parliamentary scene. It is therefore very clearly a metaphorical usage when such language is employed. However, in the Roman empire in which Paul lived—and this after all was the letter to the Romans—the literal use of the sword was common. It was part of the normal weaponry of a Roman legionary used not only in foreign conquests but also in suppressing any domestic civil unrest. So while it is vivid language to speak of the government bearing the sword, it is too close to the actual physical means employed to be so easily dismissed as simply picture language. Roman swords were used to inflict wounds and death, and Paul surely is speaking of something much more drastic than a prison sentence.

This is confirmed by his own attitude seen when he was himself on trial before a Roman governor. After his long detention by Felix he appeared before Festus. Judging by Paul's introductory remarks as he made his defence, he was much more likely to receive from Festus the fair trial which Roman justice claimed to give but which corrupt judges like Felix failed to offer. Paul recognised the seriousness of the charge against him, though he declared himself to be 'not guilty'. He also recognised the validity of a judge imposing a sentence. His words are therefore all the more significant: 'If, however, I am guilty of doing anything deserving death, I do not refuse to die' (Acts 25:11).

There are two important elements in this brief statement. In the first place, Paul recognised that there is such a thing as a crime which makes the offender liable to the death penalty. Furthermore, he viewed this penalty not as something imposed by the arbitrary whim of a judge but as the appropriate penalty. The phrase 'deserving death' is identical with the words used in the verdict of Agrippa and Festus that Paul was not guilty (Acts 26:31). They also appear in the declared verdict of Pilate concerning Jesus that he had done nothing 'to deserve death' (Lk 23:15). Paul then thus simply reinforced his recognition of the rightness of the death penalty when he added, 'I do not refuse to die.'

Paul of course had as his Bible the Old Testament. He therefore was very familiar with the book of Genesis and the story of the Flood. It was after that terrible judgement, when in fact God imposed the death penalty on a massive scale, that God made his covenant with Noah and his descendants. It included the solemn indictment of murder as the supreme crime for which the killer is to pay with the forfeiture of his own life: 'Whoever sheds the blood of man, by man shall his blood be shed; for in the image of God has God made man' (Gen 9:6).

It will not do to try and argue that this is an Old Testament rule which has been superseded by the New Testament. We are not dealing here with the ceremonial law or the ritual of the Temple which of course were superseded. We are not in the area of rabbinic interpretation which Jesus again and again modified or even rejected. We are in fact looking at one of the significant steps in the establishing of the covenant of grace, that intimate relationship which God has made with his people. It is thus an abiding truth for all time.

This conviction is reinforced by the appeal to 'the image of God' and so to the original creation of Adam. It was this image which not only made man the apex of God's creative handiwork, but stressed his unique position before his Creator. It is because of that image that men and women have the ability to think and plan, to act creatively in art and music, to have a moral urge reflecting the righteousness of the God who made them, and above all to be summoned to worship God and to enjoy fellowship with him.

It is possible to interpret Paul's words here in two different ways, but in either case the conclusion is the same. We may take them to mean that man has such a special role as the representation in flesh and blood of the invisible God that he alone dare act as judge and carry out such an awesome sentence which is ultimately the sentence pronounced by the eternal Judge.

It seems to me the more likely interpretation of his words is that Paul is emphasising the enormity of the crime of murder. It is not only a heinous crime in that it robs a fellow being of what is the most precious possession, that is life itself, and also robs family and friends of a great treasure. It is even more serious because it is an assault on God's handiwork and indeed particularly outrageous because it is a defiant rejection of God's plan when he created men and women in his own likeness. Such an appalling crime is really a blasphemy since it is not only the gravest insult to human society but a defiant insult to God himself. Only the enormity of capital punishment is an adequate reply.

This appeal to the image of God also stresses that this is no temporary decree. It does not belong to the kind of arrangements governing the worship of Israel since these clearly were transient as the letter to the Hebrews pointed out. The reality of God's image in man is, however, the great abiding fact. It is so much at the very heart of man's constitution that apart from it true humanity would not exist. The image is as much a fact in the twentieth century as it was for Noah's immediate descendants. The penalty for violating it is as binding now as it was then.

10

War

War is brutal, ugly and sordid. There is nothing glamorous or romantic in the wholesale slaughter of other human beings. Yet in the past there has often been a romanticising of warfare which has drawn attention away from the carnage and indeed was probably designed for that purpose. There is no beauty in the spectacle of mangled bodies or rotting corpses. There is no romance in the shattered lives of those who have survived the battlefield, but who live out their days in a twilight world of permanent disability or mental disintegration. The striking military uniforms in peace time, the stirring martial music, the trooping of the colour—all these present a grand spectacle. They obscure, however, the hideous reality which today is even more horrible since the advent of total war involves not only military personnel but civilian populations of both sexes and of every age group.

In view of all this it may seem quite a straightforward matter to decide the issue as to whether or not a Christian can take part in war. Surely it is completely ruled out for anyone claiming to be a disciple of the Prince of Peace? To belong to a kingdom whose basic principle is love, and in which national and tribal divisions are irrelevant, is surely to be precluded from indulging in the hate and fury of war?

In fact the problem is not so easily solved. Indeed it has been an issue over which Christians have differed down the centuries and over which they still differ. It is not that some see war as a glorious crusade and others view it as repugnant, since both may be united in their revulsion. The division comes when the debate moves to consider whether or not there are further compelling reasons leading to acceptance of war as an ugly necessity.

The pacifist, whether Christian or not, has no hesitation in rejecting war altogether as a means of deciding disputes or even of national self-defence. To mention this position is to require a distinction to be drawn between the conscientious objector and the pacifist. The two positions may seem inter-changable with both holding the same views. This, however, is not always so and it is important to notice the distinction, even if it makes little difference in practice.

The conscientious objector to military service is facing the issue of his own conscience. He comes to the conclusion that as far as he is concerned it would be wrong for him. He may as a consequence face prison and in some countries even death. These, however, he would consider the cost of Christian discipleship as far as he is concerned. Better, he would argue, to be a martyr for conscience sake than to purchase freedom at the cost of violating the authority of that insistent inner voice. Yet he would still maintain that he is not legislating for other Christians. This is one of these problem areas where believers come to different conclusions. To him the issue is clear, but he does not lay down his conviction as obligatory for all.

The pacifist goes further. He is agreed with the conscientious objector that he cannot possibly contemplate taking part in war. He argues, however, that this is not simply his own personal conviction, but is rather the only option open to the Christian who wishes to be consistent. He realises that other Christians come to different conclusions, but he is not able to accept that it is simply a matter for the individual conscience. He has to maintain that they are mistaken. He may admit that they are endeavouring to be honest in their thinking and are trying to follow the teaching of Scripture. Yet nonetheless he must still argue that they are in error. Sincere they may be. Sincere indeed they evidently are. Sincerely wrong, however, he judges them to be.

Turning to the other side, it is not a question of militaristic Christians exulting in war in a jingoistic way. Rather it is a case of troubled hearts and perplexed minds struggling with problems which may seem to the pacifist to be so easily solved, but to many Christians are much more complex. A major reason for the unreadiness to accept the pacifist argument, even while sympathising deeply with it, lies within the Bible itself. The Christian does not simply read his New Testament, but accepts a complete Bible. He recalls that for Jesus the Scriptures he delighted to quote are the books of the Old Testament. It was the same for the early Christians. When Paul wrote to Timothy and stressed the sufficiency of the Scriptures for living, it was the Old Testament which was his Bible. It was a Bible adequate for the purpose of leading a Christian to maturity: 'All Scripture is God-breathed and is useful for teaching, rebuking, correcting and training in righteousness, so that the man of God may be thoroughly equipped for every good work' (2 Tim 3:16–17).

Now it is clear beyond any contradiction that war is not only present in the history of God's people in the Old Testament, but it is fully accepted and indeed sometimes commanded by God himself. Read in Hebrews 11 and the roll call of the great men and women of faith in the Old Testament and there are names whose military prowess and victories were seen as marks of their greatness—Gideon, Barak, Samson, Jephthah, David. Go back to the stories of Joshua and Judges with Israel carrying out wholesale slaughter at the express command of the Lord. Turn to the books of the Kings and the Chronicles and it is the same pattern. It is summed up in the exultation of Moses: 'The Lord is a warrior; the Lord is his name' (Exod 15:3). An echo of that rings out in the Psalms: 'Let the saints rejoice in this honour and sing for joy on their beds. May the praise of God be in their mouths and a double-edged sword in their hands, to inflict vengeance on the nations and punishment on the peoples' (Ps 149:5–7).

A famous heretic of the second century called Marcion tried to settle the problem by teaching that the God of the Old

Testament was a different being from the God of the New Testament. One might reply by asking where was the true God and what was he doing during those stormy centuries? In fact Mercion's position is untenable since Jesus and the apostles accepted without question the continuity of the two covenants. The old covenant was old only in the sense of being preparatory to its fulfilment in the new. The God of Abraham, Isaac and Jacob; the God of the judges, the kings and the prophets is the God and Father of our Lord Jesus Christ.

In attempting to give some reply, and I hope a biblically-orientated reply, to this massive problem, we will need to go back to the record of the Fall in Genesis 3. Adam's disobedience was not merely a personal disaster since he was there as the representative man and was acting on behalf of his posterity. Thus not only was he expelled from Eden and not only was his nature corrupted, but he led the human race to ruin. Indeed, it was not only humanity which was so disastrously affected, for the very earth came under a judgement not to be revoked until the ushering in by God of 'a new heaven and a new earth, the home of righteousness' (2 Pet 3:13).

This means that in all God's dealings with men and women in subsequent history he has always been dealing with a fallen race in a corrupted environment. This meant that as he began to reveal himself, the long slow story of this revelation took place not in a perfect situation but with a fallen people. God met people where they were and made himself known to them by a self-disclosure which came in the Old Testament in promises, prophecy and types and reached its climax in the coming of Christ who is the living Word.

An illustration, both of the gradual nature of this revelation and of its adjustment to the actual situation, is seen in Jesus' reference to the Mosaic ruling on divorce (Deut 24:1–4). This came, Jesus said to them, 'because your hearts were hard' (Mk 10:5). It was not the original purpose of God. The revelation from God to Adam of the reason for marriage did not include divorce, but laid down an abiding commitment. Here we see in Deuteronomy God making a concession to meet a sad condition in order to guard against the situation being made even worse.

To apply this analogy is to see that war in the Old Testament was not part of God's plan for humanity. Rather it was his tolerance of means to avoid an even greater disaster which would be the kind of mass slaughter seen in Hitler's genocidal plans executed in the concentration camps. There are strong indications within the Old Testament that war is still a tolerated necessity which will one day be eliminated with the final elimination of sin and of Satan.

Thus David who is presented as the greatest of the kings and a great man of God was excluded from the privilege of building the Temple. God acknowledged that it was good that he had the desire. Nevertheless God insisted, 'You have shed much blood and have fought many wars. You are not to build a house for my Name, because you have shed much blood on the earth in my sight' (1 Chron 22:8). God had helped him in his battles and given him the victory. Indeed, some of his Psalms reflect his gratitude for that help. Yet at best his wars were not such great achievements. They were tolerated, but they left such a stain that the pure worship of God in the Temple must not be compromised by association with them.

The same attitude to war is seen in the prophetic vision of the glorious future peace when wars shall for ever have ended: 'They will beat their swords into ploughshares and their spears into pruning hooks. Nation will not take up sword against nation, nor will they train for war any more' (Is 2:4). Isaiah fully accepted the international situation as it was in his day. He was alongside Hezekiah the king, reassuring him in face of the military threat of Assyria. Yet at the same time he recognised that war and defence of the realm belonged to this imperfect age. In the coming glory of the Lord's return, war like sickness and death and all the other manifestations of sin would be banished from God's universe.

Even within the permissive providence of God which tolerated war, there are still restraints. So there are rules for the treatment of captives and also stern words in face of atrocities. Oded the prophet meets Pekah, the king of the northern kingdom, who had just defeated Judah. That battle was in fact the declared judgement of God as the prophet Oded declared to the King: 'Because the Lord, the God of your fathers, was angry with Judah, he gave them into your hand' (2 Chron 28:9). That however did not give Pekah a licence to commit atrocities. So the prophet adds the stern rebuke: 'But you have slaughtered them in a rage that reaches to heaven.'

Turning then to the New Testament, we find indeed the era of fulfilled prophecies, substance in place of shadow, completeness in place of preparation, goals instead of anticipation. Yet with all the newness of the new covenant there is still a continuity. God has not changed his character. He has not adjusted his standards. There are different patterns in his working, but there is no moral contradiction between old patterns and new methods.

The man who may be seen as bestriding the frontier between the old and the new was John the Baptist. He lived as a contemporary of Jesus and indeed gladly saw his own disciples move to a greater allegiance as they followed the Messiah whom it was John's ministry to glorify. Yet still he belonged more to the Old Testament prophets, since his life and ministry were essentially preparatory and ended before the great climactic events of Calvary and the resurrection. It was as a man embracing the old and the new that he spoke to the soldiers who came to him. Members of an occupying army, yet responding to a Jewish prophet, they were clearly moved by his trumpet call to repentance. They asked him: 'What should we do?' In his reply there was no hint that they were in an untenable position as soldiers. There was no suggestion that they would have to leave the army. Instead the requirements were practical and in terms of how they should behave in their continuing military role: 'Don't extort money and don't accuse people falsely—be content with your pay' (Lk 3:14).

Jesus adopted a similar stance as far as soldiers were concerned. There is the remarkable story of the Roman centurion who came to ask for healing for his servant—remarkable for the quality of faith which he exhibited. Again there was no hint of a rebuke for his role as an officer in the army and no suggestion that he should aim to quit. Rather Jesus concentrated on the strength of faith shown: 'I tell you the truth, I have not found anyone in Israel with such great faith' (Mt 8:10).

Both Matthew and Luke record without any qualification the reaction of the centurion at the cross. This tough Roman soldier was in charge of the brutal procedure and had doubtless been involved in many other similar executions. Yet he was overwhelmed by the wonder of the dying Jesus and was moved to the confession: 'Surely he was the Son of God . . . Surely this was a righteous man' (Mt 27:54; Lk 23:47). Luke emphasises that this was not some involuntary exclamation or some superstitious reaction, by adding that the centurion 'praised God' as he spoke.

The Acts reflects this same attitude to Roman troops—grateful acknowledgement of their faith or of their constructive attitudes, coupled with a total absence of any questioning of their continuing in the army. One of the most significant steps forward in the spread of the gospel was the opening of the door of faith to the Gentiles. It was such a major new chapter that many Jewish Christians found it very hard to accept. Even Peter required a direct revelation from God before he could bring himself to accept Gentiles as converts. In the context of our present discussion on war, it is significant that the man God chose to be the catalyst to precipitate this great change, was a Roman soldier. Cornelius the centurion was already known as 'devout and God-fearing; he gave generously to those in need and prayed to God regularly' (Acts 10:2). He exhibited a great readiness to respond to the light he already had and to react eagerly to the possibilities of a more complete revelation from God. God's testimony to the genuineness of his faith was striking. 'The Holy Spirit came on all who heard the message' (Acts 10:44). Great was the surprise of Jewish Christians who had come with Peter 'for they heard them speaking in tongues and praising God' (Acts 10:46). Subsequently, Peter had to defend his action before the Jewish believers in Jerusalem. Their concern was that he 'went into the house of uncircumcised men and ate with them' (Acts 11:2), but neither on the memorable occasion at Caesarea, nor at the subsequent encounter in Jerusalem, was there any critical mention of the fact that the particular Gentile at the heart of the controversy was a soldier and an officer at that!

Of even greater significance was Paul's dealings with Roman soldiers. He owed much to them. They rescued him from the Jewish mob which was bent on murdering him in Jerusalem (Acts 21:31). His life was again saved by the prompt action of the troops when the sailors were about to abandon the ship and its passengers off Malta and again, very shortly afterwards, it was only the authority of the centurion and his prompt readiness to face a breakdown of discipline which kept Paul intact.

However, the most significant incident as far as the issue of this chapter is concerned, was Paul's appeal for military protection against the plot to kill him hatched by some extremist Jews. These potential killers had the backing of the chief priests and elders as they planned to get Paul away from the protection of the army for a supposed further interrogation. When Paul got wind of this via his nephew he had no hesitation in asking one of the centurions to take the young man to the commander to report the assassination attempt. Clearly he was glad to have the protection of a very heavily armed escort of both infantry and cavalry.

The earlier incidents might be dismissed as irrelevant by some who might possibly argue that Paul was simply accepting the protection offered without any endorsement of the means employed. Even were we to accept that interpretation, which incidentally ignores Paul's active involvement with the centurion on the ship, this appeal to the army commander is much more indisputably relevant. Paul knew clearly what was involved. These troops were well armed. They were in a turbulent province and would certainly not have had the slightest hesitation in dispatching any band of Jewish assassins. He was thus making his appeal to the use of military force. If Paul was a pacifist, then this was a grossly inconsistent if not hypocritical action. You cannot at one and the same time reject the possibility of war and yet appeal for personal protection to troops ready to use armed force to ensure that protection.

This incident indeed strongly reinforces the view I expressed earlier in discussing capital punishment, that the sword wielded by the state (Rom 13:4) was no symbolic bauble. For Paul, the sword of the state was to be drawn for the protection of the citizen and when he himself was in extreme danger he was ready to appeal to state force for his protection. So both his letter to Rome and his own conduct are consistent with each other. When later he wrote the great passage on spiritual warfare in Ephesians 6, the detail of the armour worn by the Roman soldier had a special meaning for him as he could look back to that night when he was ringed by steel as armed men responded to his request and escorted him safely to Caesarea.

All this seems to point towards the acceptance of war as an ugly reality in a fallen world where the ambitions of godless men will only falter in face of force or the threat of force. We are not, however, freed from every problem by accepting this position, since it is often very difficult to decide who is the aggressor because truth is one of the earliest casualties. Where, however, the issue is clear and one's own nation is obviously in the wrong, then it would be as wrong for a Christian to support the war effort on the basis of accepting the authority of the state, as it would be for a son to obey his father because it is scriptural if in fact the father wanted his son to join him in theft!

This morning before I wrote these pages there was a striking illustration of this very issue in the morning newspapers. A young white South African was sentenced to six years' imprisonment for refusing to accept his military call up. Though his was the longest sentence yet handed out, he was not the first to take this stand. Not all these objectors have been pacifists. However, they have drawn a firm distinction between being ready to serve their country and being willing to repress and kill black fellow countrymen in the cause of maintaining the iniquities of apartheid.

There are further problems associated first of all with the issue of killing the innocent and to a supremely greater degree with the ultimate horrors of nuclear war. One might conceivably argue that in war the death of innocent victims is virtually unavoidable and represents one of war's greatest tragedies—there must have been many infants and children in Canaan not personally responsible for the vileness of their parents, but who perished in the slaughter commanded by God. It is quite another matter when, for example, in the use of modern aerial bombardment, whole cities are deliberately reduced to ruins as was Dresden in the second world war with consequent massive loss of life. This becomes an even more horrific prospect in face of possible nuclear warfare, as it is not only the living who are killed or maimed, but generations yet unborn who would be tragically malformed because of genetic damage due to radiation. One therefore has to ask very insistently if these do not constitute the kinds of atrocity which is an offence not only to humanity but also to heaven. One hears again the Old Testament rebuke noted earlier when Oded challenged Pekah after his massacre of the people of Judah.

There is an important qualification which needs to be added to all this discussion in view of the fact that emotional language can easily cloud clear thinking. Thus reference may be made to the sum total of human suffering as if it was something to be quantified or measured. In fact the sum total of any human suffering is that which can be endured by any one individual. The idea may be contemplated of a multiplication of human suffering to the n'th degree, producing a vast reservoir of pain. In fact such an idea exists only in the imagination. To note this qualification is not in any way to try and minimise the horrors of widespread suffering and death. It is simply to aim at clarity of thought so that we can focus on the enormity of a nuclear holocaust where the pain of individuals is intense and where that pain is repeated so many times that our minds become numb with horror.

One may therefore argue that there is nothing ultimately different between any forms of warfare which produce the same effects of suffering, grief and death. There is the same ugliness in a tribal fight with fifty casualties and an international conflict with fifty million casualties. One might also argue that either war is totally wrong or that there is no limit to be placed on the means used. What difference is there in the final analysis between a man dying from radiation sickness, chemical weapons or gangrene as a result of gunshot wounds. The net result is the same and the possible accompaniments are alike—indeed sudden nuclear annihilation is at least painless in contrast with a lingering death on some remote battlefield.

One comes round in a circle to the starting point. We are not living as yet in the full realisation of the kingdom of heaven. We are in a fallen world. In John's words: 'We know that we are children of God, and that the whole world is under the control of the evil one' (1 Jn 5:19). Christians are a tiny minority, even in nations which in some vague way claim adherence to the Christian faith. They are an even tinier minority in many other lands where Christ is totally rejected or ignored.

They are not therefore cast in the role of the decision-makers or the national leaders. They must therefore learn how to live in a world whose laws often diverge from the standards they find in the Bible, whose materialistic concerns and plans are remote from the unselfishness of the biblical pattern and whose wars reflect so much of human sinfulness, selfishness and greed. It is because we are citizens at one and the same time of two kingdoms, one heavenly and one earthly, that life presents us with such complex problems. Often we have to opt not for the ideal but for the least objectionable path in the particular situation in which we live. The issue of war is one of the most acute of these problems of trying to live as good citizens, while yet avoiding compromise or denial of the faith.

There is a sense in which we are forced into an involuntary compromise by our very citizenship. Our taxes are used for some purposes at least that we would certainly not support if we had the choice. We cannot even take the step which some have taken of withholding part of our tax as part of a protest say against nuclear arms. Taxation has in any case become so pervasive with VAT that in many of the ordinary purchases, whether of goods or services, we are supporting the government's policies. While war or preparation for possible war makes this involuntary involvement more painful, it does also confront us with the opportunity of action. So if war comes, the potential combatant may either accept the implications of citizenship or he may for conscience sake refuse to fight and face the consequences.

Even in the case of refusal to fight there are other consequences apart from immediate penalties. I recall a conscientious objector who was clearly a sensitive man expressing what to him was a great personal problem. He recognised that peace in Britain and deliverance from the horrors of Hitler's tyranny were purchased by the blood of those who fought and died to maintain their country's freedom. The pain for him was that he was enjoying the benefits which they had won at such cost to themselves, while he could not conscientiously follow them. To be a beneficiary of others' sacrifice which one does not and will not face is undoubtedly a painful experience.

In this whole vexed issue, Christians clearly come to different conclusions. For some, submission as in Romans 13 to the authority of the state involves the grim necessity of military service. For others, the consideration of love for others and obedience to what is seen as the will of God are overriding considerations. For both sides the next chapter of Romans is especially important. There Paul deals with the matter of conscientious differences between Christians. They may be equally committed to the lordship of Christ and equally desirous to follow Scripture and yet they differ markedly in some area of conduct. The natural reaction is for one to stand in judgement on the other, and for the other to respond with contempt at the person's apparent bondage, as it seems to him. Paul is very clear: 'Who are you to judge someone else's servant? To his own master he stands or falls ... for we will all stand before God's judgement seat' (Rom 14:4,10). In this agonising dilemma in face of war, we must respect each other's conscience and aim to do what we believe is acceptable to our God. 'Blessed is the man who does not condemn himself by what he approves' (Rom 14:22). Meantime, the summons is to prayer that God may give us peace in our time and spare us both the horrors of war and the consequent anguished decisions of conscience.

11

The Welfare State

Comprehensive welfare arrangements have become so much part of everyday life that it is difficult to realise that the welfare state in its British form is not much over forty years old. It is true that there were earlier attempts to meet the problem of poverty. The old age pension dates from the early years of this century and the poor law goes right back to the time of the first Elizabeth. However, the concept of a complete scheme of social welfare is comparatively recent.

In spite of different emphases it has been the common policy of all three major political parties. The formulation by Lord Beveridge in his famous report came from a liberal. The first step in implementing the scheme came through the coalition at the end of the second world war. The major development came under the post-war Labour government with the outstanding plan of a National Health Service free to all, with need rather than financial resource being the determining factor. It has in the succeeding years been developed by both Conservative and Labour governments who have continued to pledge their commitment.

More recently there has been a breakdown of the earlier political consensus. On the one hand there have been attempts to modify schemes of state welfare and on the other hand protests that the welfare state is subtly being dismantled. It is not however part of the purpose of this book to take sides in the party political debate. Rather I want to look at the idea of state welfare in general and then to consider some of the implications and dangers from a Christian point of view.

Certainly there is a strong biblical emphasis throughout both the Old and New Testament on the responsibility of caring for the weak and the poor. In the Old Testament the widow, the fatherless, the poor and the foreigner were all the objects of concern, and a substantial part of the levitical law was directed towards them.

To see others in need and to fail to come to their aid was a very serious matter, as Job recognised so clearly when he protested his innocence:

> If I have denied the desires of the poor or let the eyes of the widow grow weary, if I have kept my bread to myself, not sharing it with the fatherless . . . if I have seen anyone perish for lack of clothing, or a needy man without a garment, and his heart did not bless me for warming him with the fleece from my sheep, if I have raised my hand against the fatherless, knowing that I had influence in court, then let my arm fall from the shoulder, let it be broken off at the joint (Job 31:16–22).

Isaiah has a stern word of God's judgement on the leaders of the nation. A major reason is their callous indifference to the needs of the weak and their 'grinding the faces of the poor' (Is 3:15). Amos, the prophet of national judgement, indicts Israel. Again and again in his words of denunciation he returns to the same charge. He sees wealth, ease and luxury, but these have been purchased at the expense of the needy. It is no wonder that he blazes with passionate indignation at those who 'trample on the heads of the poor as upon the dust of the ground and deny justice to the oppressed' (Amos 2:7; also 4:1; 5:11–12; 8:4–6).

Judah went through God's judgement as both their land and their capital fell to the Babylonian army and they went into exile. They experienced the amazing grace of God in their return from exile to their own land. Yet still the prophets have to summon them to repentance for their sins. Again the endemic selfishness and materialism of sinful men and women are evident. The message of so many of the prophets is heard again: 'This is what the Lord Almighty says: "Administer true justice and compassion to one another. Do not oppress the widow or the fatherless, the alien or the poor."'

The ministry of Jesus had that same concern. The widows and the needy were the objects of special attention. In face of one apparently potential disciple he exposed the love of riches which were to this young man such a hindrance: 'Go, sell your possessions and give to the poor, and you will have treasure in heaven' (Mt 19:21). He did not give that message to every seeker, but then everyone did not have the same obsession with wealth.

He did however insist that concern for the needy was a mark of the true disciple. Thus he told the parable of the good Samaritan who, in contrast to the priest and the Levite, showed true compassion. He also gave the sombre picture of the final day of judgement when callous indifference to others was the evidence that someone exhibiting such an attitude was no true disciple.

The early Christians followed in his footsteps. In the cruel world of the first century they exhibited a great love for others, especially those in need. It is true that they had an especial concern for their fellow believers, since persecution of the churches often left Christians facing great hardship, and so meant they were in special need. However, while Paul for example highlighted this area of concern it was within a wider summons to Christian benevolence: 'Therefore, as we have opportunity, let us do good to all people, especially to those who belong to the family of believers' (Gal 6:10).

That tradition of mercy has continued down Christian history. The Middle Ages saw in a rough and brutal age a developing care for the sick and the needy, the lepers and the outcasts. Indeed some of the great hospitals of today have their roots centuries back in Christian concern. The evangelical revival saw that concern impelled by a fresh surge of spiritual life to push forward to new areas of need. The rise of the missionary movement carried that concern to the end of the earth.

Christians, therefore, of all people should gladly welcome every opportunity to meet the needs of those who find it impossible to meet their own. The fact that the state has taken over many of the tasks which were formerly the concern of the churches must not elicit either regret or resentment. Rather it should cause delight and also produce the incentive to find ever new areas where Christian compassion can find an outlet.

It is surely totally compatible with the statement on the nature of the state in Romans 13 that the government should assume responsibilities for the provision of welfare. While there is a strong emphasis in that passage on what we might term the negative role of the state in restraining evil, there is also a clearly declared positive role. The ruler, to quote again Paul's words, 'is God's servant to do you good' (Rom 13:4). The good of the citizen surely means the welfare of the citizen.

This does not simply mean the protection of the people from the violence of the thief or the murderer. It involves protecting the weak from the economic pressures which come from forces right outside their control. It means not only providing peace for vigorous civic life, but also helping those with sickness or disability, those left in poverty because of the death of the main earner in the family, those whose marriage has been torn asunder by an unfaithful husband who leaves wife and children in poverty, those who having given a lifetime's contribution to the community have now passed beyond working age.

The Christian should have no difficulty in recognising and indeed welcoming the welfare role of the state. Our God is not only the Author of saving grace, but is also the source of general benevolence to all. When the state devises schemes which are benevolent in their care for citizens in need, it is displaying the common grace of God which has not only instituted the state, but uses his own institution to mediate his kindness to many.

While acknowledging gladly the benefits of the welfare state, the Christian will also be aware of dangers implied in such a programme. This is not to try and introduce some carping criticism by the back door. It is simply to recognise that such are human sinfulness, and thus selfishness, that every human action is liable to be deflected into wrong channels. This applies even with what may seem the most generous concerns.

Take as an illustration a parent's love for a child. That love will rightly be reflected right across the spectrum of the child's needs. We are sadly aware, however, of the spoilt child where parental love and concern have not been rightly moderated by wise discipline. The answer is not to decry parental care and it is certainly not to condone parental neglect. It is simply to keep in view a necessary qualification if excess kindness is not to become unkindness. So to add critical riders to the exercise of state welfare is in no way to suggest that the government should move out of the welfare area. It is simply to add salutary reminders of the perils of uncontrolled benevolence.

One obvious danger is that a government may be tempted to go so far down the road of caring that it ends up virtually taking over the citizen's life. Thus, instead of the very precious possession of individuality and personal freedom, men and women are reduced to the level of statistics in a faceless bureaucrat's file.

This can happen imperceptibly. Indeed it may develop in the context of increasing provision for genuine needs. In order to provide for any area of need, whether in hospitals or roads, whether in schools or in water supplies, any government needs to have knowledge. It needs to know where there are concentrations of population, what are the comparative age groups in any area, what particular epidemic illness may need to be prepared for with immunisation. So one could extend the list indefinitely and one could also acknowledge the genuine reasons for accumulating the required information.

Governments, however, are composed of ordinary sinners like the rest of us. If one needed any corroboration of this fact one only needs to read a political biography such as Michael Foot's pen portrait of Aneurin Bevan, the minister of health who introduced the National Health Service. Sin, however, in all of us means selfishness. In the politician that can easily develop in terms of desire for power. One is then reminded of the famous saying of the historian Lord Acton that all power corrupts and absolute power corrupts absolutely. We have seen in our own century where the very worthy socialist slogan 'from each according to his ability to each according to his need' led to its total perversion by Stalin in the USSR.

We are now in the computer age. No previous generation has had such an immediate access to such a vast area of information.

Never before could such a welter of statistics on such an immense scale be recorded and kept within easy access. The danger of misuse is thus even more a possibility than ever before. Since men and women have not changed, and sin and selfishness remain the same, there will always be politicians eager to exert more and more authority. The button on the computer presents them with unparalleled opportunities for moving towards absolute control.

It is wise therefore to keep a watchful eye on any development, be it ever so benevolent, which is tending to the curtailing of human liberty. Some curtailment is obviously necessary or social life would be impossible. Its extent however and perhaps even more its longer-term implications should be the object of vigilant scrutiny.

The dangers however are not only associated with the purveyors of welfare, but also with the recipients. Sin and selfishness are not the special characteristics of politicians, for they belong to all of us. It is simply that they manifest themselves in different ways. One can see this in any act of personal generosity. The donor may act generously enough and yet the giving is spoiled because of pride and smug self-satisfaction. The recipient may express grateful thanks and may indeed feel such gratitude, and yet his response is tainted by the inner feelings of envy at the financial resources of the other or of bitterness that he has not had what he would term the same good fortune.

So the recipient of state welfare needs to be aware of spiritual dangers. Clearly the man or woman with no spiritual life will not tend even to consider such issues. The Christian, however, who is called to be holy, will be on guard lest what should be a grateful response both to the state welfare agency and to the God who ordained it, becomes corrupted by accompanying sinful attitudes. To some of these we must turn.

The first area of concern is that of work. Honest toil is not an irksome necessity, but a commitment given to us by God. It is there in the story of creation where God put Adam in the Garden of Eden to tend it, and that meant work. The change which came through the Fall was that work now was accompanied by the frustrations involved in the judgement upon the created order.

Instead of the paradise of Eden there would be thorns and thistles, and all the time there would be the sobering realisation that life itself would be temporary, so that at death every achievement would be left behind.

The New Testament maintains this emphasis on work done to God's glory. Paul for example is very firm indeed on any pseudo-spiritual arguments to buttress a work-shy attitude: 'If a man will not work, he shall not eat' (2 Thess 3:10). Obviously he was not referring to a situation where work was not available, but to a straight issue of idleness. Work, and in this he included manual labour, is a means whereby a Christian glorifies God. Even in the case of forced labour he counselled slaves: 'Serve wholeheartedly, as if you were serving the Lord, not men' (Eph 6:7).

This biblical emphasis on the dignity of work leads to two conclusions. On the one hand a government is failing in its responsibilities if it does not aim to provide opportunities of work for all. Admittedly in the rapidly changing complexity of modern technological society it is not always easy to achieve this goal. Some of the economic factors may be completely outside any one particular government's control. The goal however should be there and we must insist that workers are never to be viewed as mere items on an economic graph. They are creatures of the working Creator, and being made in his image need the fulfilment of work to enable them to realise their divinely-given potential.

On the other side of the work issue is the attitude of the worker. Welfare payments are intended to help in times of need. They are not designed to give the opportunity to drop out of society. Those who claim to adopt an alternative lifestyle while living on state benefit are not idealists but loafers, and need to be seen as such. The Christian can have no part in such an attitude.

An allied problem is the difficult choice when the gap between pay and unemployment is so small that from a purely material point of view there is little incentive to find a job. The Christian with a true view of work cannot follow this line since work is not merely a wage-producing activity, but a trust given by God.

At the same time comment surely is needed on the role of

government. To countenance the existence of such a slight financial margin is to deprive people of the incentive to work. The answer to this is not to depress unemployment benefit even further in order to force people to look for work. Rather it is a case of dealing by law with the selfishness of the employer by insisting on a statutory minimum wage.

In any relationship where one side is the provider and the other is the receiver there is the danger of developing a dependency mentality. Parents have to watch this with their teenage children, some of whom will cheerfully go along with provision without demands. Such are not likely to learn either the real value of money or the cost of earning it. So the welfare state can degenerate into a cushioned society whose aim is that any hardship should be eliminated. That can also eliminate personal incentive. It is not always easy to work out the solution. God certainly has it well worked out in his requirements for Christian living. The alternatives are neither 'let go and let God', nor massive personal effort. It is rather a balanced combination of both: 'Work out your salvation with fear and trembling, for it is God who works in you to will and to act according to his good purpose' (Phil 2:12). There is a principle here which has a wider application. In the matter of provision for others, the aim should be to provide what is necessary without dulling the incentive of the recipient. On the latter's part the response should be to receive needed resources with thanksgiving, not as an excuse for slackness, but as a stimulus to use every resource to realise our full humanity.

One area of special concern in the whole debate on state welfare is the life of the family. The family unit is even more basic in God's plan for humanity than is the state. Indeed one could argue that the family unit was part of the original design in creation. The state was also God's gracious provision, but only subsequent to the Fall which in bringing sin into the world brought also the need for state control.

Wherever government activity threatens the well-being of the family, the Christian and the church should be alert to resist such encroachment. In South Africa for example the most grievous aspect of apartheid is its destructive effects on family life. To force black people to live in separate areas is to drive a wedge between the wage earner and the family. To have a mother working in a white area and forced by the Group Areas Act to live apart from her children is a scandalous evil. To force a man to spend most of his year in his wage-earning capacity far from his wife and children is again a grievous evil and one which calls for protest.

The Christian's voice also needs to be heard in welfare arrangements where the caring agencies of the local city council usurp the role of the parents. Indeed, as was seen in the Cleveland episode, the laudable aim of protecting children from sexual abuse led to the grievous wrong of separating children from their parents who were subsequently adjudged innocent.

When a council uses the rates paid by the citizens to propagate teaching subversive of marriage, it is time to protest. When the government seems ready to give way to the highly-organised and well-financed lobby wanting seven-day shop opening, it is important to plead for the family. If the one day when a mother can be with her children is filched by those greedy for profit, the government responsible for legalising such a change needs to be made aware that they are attacking the very fabric of society.

A further cause for concern is the careless attitude to state facilities and property. Too many people view it as simply a matter of being sufficiently clever to beat the system. Others think of the state in such vague and impersonal terms that they do not reckon that misusing state funds or manipulating state welfare belongs to the same category as stealing a neighbour's purse or vandalising a neighbour's house.

One final danger may be noted, and it is one which is of particular significance and concern for Christians. It is that state welfare can lead to a mentality that security and comfort are the supreme goals of life. While it is true as Jesus willingly conceded that we need food, clothes and homes, and while our heavenly Father knows we need them, yet there are other considerations. The Father who has this concern for our welfare is the God who sent his Son, yet Jesus did not have a home of his own and ended his brief life buried in a borrowed tomb.

The sad dearth of missionary recruits is a comment on the subtle spread of materialism in the churches. The current mentality of the world is, 'What's in this for me?' The present stress on security easily becomes the dominant concern. The attitude of the earlier missionary pioneers was rather in terms of grateful thanks for all God's provisions, coupled with a glad readiness to give all in the service of the Saviour, even life itself.

Jesus felt great pity for the crowds who were hungry and by his miraculous power he fed them. He was stirred with compassion when he saw the ravages of leprosy or the grievous handicap of physical disability, and he brought healing. His life and his ministry reflected his concern for the whole person, both body and soul. Yet always there was the even higher consideration which was the glory of God.

It is the vision of this glory being reflected in human lives which has led countless Christians down the centuries to follow Paul as he wrote: 'But whatever was to my profit I now consider loss for the sake of Christ' (Phil 3:7). Paul however wrote and acted as he did, and the other disciples acted as they did, because of the ultimate challenge of Christ himself:

> So do not worry, saying, 'What shall we eat?' or 'What shall we drink?' or 'What shall we wear?' For the pagans run after all these things, and your heavenly Father knows that you need them. But seek first his kingdom and his righteousness, and all these things will be given to you as well (Mt 6:31–33).

Notes

1. Clerical Disabilities Act 1870 (33 and 34 Vict. C 91) Disestablishment and Disendowment of the Church of Ireland 1871.
2. F J Foakes-Jackson, *The History of the Christian Church to AD 461* (Deighton Bell & Co Ltd, 1942), p 89.
3. Conor Cruise O'Brien, *States of Ireland* (Panther Books Ltd, 1974), p 288.
4. John Calvin, *Institutes of the Christian Religion* (James Clarke & Co, 1949), Book iv, chap xx, para 32.
5. Emil Brunner, *The Divine Imperative* (Lutterworth Press, 1942), p 477.

Letters From A Soviet Prison Camp

by Mikhail Khorev

'Whenever I think of my friends and fellow believers who have suffered some of the worst punishment in prisons and penal camps for Christ's sake, I think above all of Mikhail Ivanovich Khorev. May the life, service and sufferings of our beloved brother Mikhail be a source of blessing to many readers.' GEORGI VINS

This book contains the first account in English of the trial of Mikhail Khorev, a leader of the (unregistered) Evangelical Baptists in the Soviet Union, along with 33 letters from prison to his sons that were secretly printed in the USSR. They form a moving account of one man's sufferings for Christ and a challenging masterpiece of Christian spirituality.

MIKHAIL KHOREV is currently free, working in secret for the Church and constantly risking arrest. He is married with three sons, one of whom has also been imprisoned for his faith.

Monarch
Publications